# THE HONDA VALKYRIE

## PETER RAKESTROW

AMBERLEY

First published 2017

Amberley Publishing
The Hill, Stroud,
Gloucestershire, GL5 4EP

www.amberley-books.com

ISBN: 978 1 4456 7486 5 (print)
ISBN: 978 1 4456 7487 2 (ebook)

British Library Cataloguing in Publication Data.
A catalogue record for this book is available from the British Library.

Typeset in 10pt on 13pt Celeste.
Origination by Amberley Publishing.
Printed in the UK.

# Contents

Introduction          5

1 The Man and his Dream          7

2 The Concept          12

3 Power Cruisers          18

4 Reinvention of the Interstate          54

5 Rune: From Concept to Reality          66

6 Gold Wing Valkyrie/F6C          84

Acknowledgements          96

*To Caroll & Larry*

*Best wishes*

*Peter R*

# Introduction

In the motorcycle's heyday, there were hundreds of manufacturers all over the world, but they were just producing motorcycles. Special terms for different motorcycle categories hadn't been invented, until, that is, Honda introduced the CB750. The world's first 'Superbike', this fast, clean machine was smooth and high revving.

Gradually, owners and companies would add items like fairings and saddlebags, which made machines deliver a different style of riding experience, but 'Tourer' wasn't a term used for such machines in the 1940s and '50s. In the '60s, owners customising their bikes was a big thing; take a Triumph, change the frame, extend the forks and fit a large rear tyre – also fit high handlebars, making the machine uncomfortable to ride and not handle that well, but hey, 'I have a 'chopper', you don't!'

One manufacturer in particular that has evolved into these sorts of motorcycles is Harley-Davidson; they have developed a following for their motorcycles offering laid-back style machines that could easily be modified to the owner's taste, 'Captain America, Easy-Rider' style.

In the early 1970s, Honda was trying to build a machine that would serve two purposes – a Sports bike and a Touring bike (dubbed the 'M1') – but the market wasn't ready for such a machine. By then Harley-Davidson did have a Tourer – the Electro-glide – but it wasn't until 1980 with the Honda Gold Wing Interstate that the term 'Tourer' really stuck. It was the 1980s that gave the industry such terms as 'Sports bikes', 'Touring bikes' and then, later, 'Customs', categorising the different motorcycle styles. Then, in 1985, Yamaha released the awesome 'V-Max', introducing a new motorcycle category altogether – the 'Hot Rod' or 'Muscle bike'. This, along with Kawasaki's ZL900 Eliminator, was in response to Honda's Magna series, a V4-engined custom.

The Japanese manufacturers were now making machines with low seat heights, high-rise pulled back handlebars, teardrop fuel tanks, and rider foot pegs positioned further forward. Engines were generally detuned for a more sedate ride when just cruising down the highway; it didn't matter what type of engine was used, although Harley-Davidson was deemed to be the ideal custom cruiser with its 'V-twin' engine.

In the '90s, Japanese manufacturers were producing a variety of machines that seemed to be Harley lookalikes with V-twin engines. Even Honda got in on the act with their VT series of V-twins, which became more commonly known as 'Cruisers' rather than 'Customs', but it wasn't until the mid-90s that Honda built the first 'Power Cruiser'.

Enter the Honda GL1500 Valkyrie; this long, heavy, cruising machine created a whole new motorcycle category of its own. From its opposed six-cylinder engine and six carburettors to its retro-looking front and rear mudguards, it was a massive machine with lashings of chrome. The Valkyrie was also fitted with large front and rear tyres, a bulbous fuel tank, and a long six-into-six exhaust system.

Having three versions of the GL1500 Valkyrie – the standard Valkyrie/F6C, Valkyrie Tourer and Valkyrie Interstate from 1997 to 2003 – Honda was really getting into the 'Power Cruiser' market. Then, in 2003, Honda released the first concept bike for mass production – the NRX1800 Valkyrie Rune. This went on sale as a 2004 and 2005 model. In 2014, nine years after the Rune, Honda produced the GL1800 Gold Wing Valkyrie/F6C, a stripped-down version of the Gold Wing Tourer.

The Honda 1,520cc horizontally opposed six-cylinder engine, originally fitted into the 1988 GL1500 Gold Wing, was adapted and modified for the GL1500 Valkyrie/F6C. The 2014 GL1800 Gold Wing Valkyrie's 1,832cc engine is the same as that fitted to the GL1800 Gold Wing.

In all its guises, the Valkyrie epitomises Honda's advertising slogans, from the 1990s' 'Come Ride With Us', to the more recent 'The Power Of Dreams'.

## 'Spirit of the Phoenix'

'An upright position to enjoy cruising. Low and long styling to give a strong presence. High quality that fulfils a sense of ownership and finally a vehicle that gives the rider the same feeling of connection as a rider and horse. Honda has called this spirit of making motorcycles.' 'The Spirit of the Phoenix'.

# 1

# The Man and his Dream

Everyone has dreams, but not everyone's dreams become reality. One man, however, with both the ambition and determination to make his dreams come true, created a company that was successful, although at times nearly faulted. That man was Soichiro Honda. Born to a blacksmith in 1906 in a small village called Komyo in Japan, the eldest son only had eight years of formal education and graduated in 1922. Soichiro was a practical person, not interested in book learning, and at the age of sixteen took an apprenticeship in Tokyo to learn more about the thing he loved most, the motor car. On finishing his apprenticeship, he returned to Hamamatsu to open his own car repair shop; after a number of years the business had become lucrative and Honda, with his newfound wealth, became a bit of a playboy and started racing cars. After winning a few races he realised that he wasn't just successful in business but racing as well. Unfortunately, his racing career was cut short due to an accident at the All-Japan speed rally when a car suddenly pulled across his path at 100 mph. Honda was badly hurt and he took eighteen months to recover.

After Soichiro Honda's recovery, at the age of thirty he decided to start a new business. This was to make piston rings as he thought they were a commodity with repeat business. He employed fifty people, borrowed cash, and bought a factory, but his luck was running out and the business turned into a disaster; his money was diminishing and he couldn't find the right formula to make a successful ring. After this episode in his life Soichiro decided he needed to know more so enrolled himself on a course at the Hamamatsu Institute of Technology to learn about metallurgy. As in his early school years, Honda wasn't interested in the textbook approach and had a cavalier attitude, only attending the lectures he thought were worthwhile. One day the institute principle, Tei Adachi, called him into his office to tell Soichiro that he was not worthy of a diploma. The unrepentant Mr Honda said: 'The diploma? That's worth less than a cinema ticket. The ticket guarantees that you can get into the cinema, but the diploma can't guarantee that you can make a living'. The professor was aghast at his comments.

Two years passed and Honda set up another company called Tokai Seiki Heavy Industries, again to make piston rings. By late November 1937 the company managed to make its first acceptable ring. His piston rings sold all over Japan but because of the Second World War male labour dried up, so Honda developed a sophisticated machine to

Soichiro Honda with marketing genius Takeo Fujisawa. (Honda)

make his piston rings that unskilled women could operate. Unfortunately, Honda's factory was heavily bombed by the Americans and in January 1945 it was completely destroyed by an earthquake. After Honda got Tokai Seiki back together again, he decided to sell the company to his biggest customer, Toyota, and after that Soichiro 'dropped-out'; he went on drinking sessions, threw parties and played his bamboo flute (the *shakuhachi*), but was still on the lookout for a new business.

By October 1946, Honda was ready to start again. This time, with the little money he had left, he established the Honda Technical Research Institute on a levelled bomb site in downtown Hamamatsu. The institute operated from a small wooden shack, which was only 18 x 12 feet. The economy was bankrupt and industry had collapsed; Japan had been virtually destroyed during the Second World War with factories and shops totally flattened. Transportation was one of the biggest problems – it was in disarray, chaotic and overcrowded. Petrol was in short supply with rationing, which meant Honda couldn't use his car and he hated being jammed in buses and trains with everybody else.

One day Honda was offered 500 surplus petrol engines that had been used by the military for generators. This gave him an idea; if he strapped an engine to a pedal-cycle and made it motorised it would make people's lives a little easier. These became so successful that the supply of engines soon began to dry up, and Honda decided that this opportunity was too good to give up, so he sat down to design and build his own petrol engine. The engine Honda developed was based on the old surplus one but, because of the petrol shortage, turpentine and petrol were mixed together. Unfortunately, this made the engine very smoky and the bike, known as the 'A-type' – a 0.5 hp 50cc two-stroke bicycle motor – was dubbed the 'Chimney'. It was then in 1948 that Honda made a new machine – the B-type, which was a 90cc version of the A-type. Orders flooded in and things progressed

Honda's first motorised bicycle, using a supply of two-stroke 50cc Tohatsu war surplus radio generator engines. (Honda)

so fast that Soichiro Honda decided to form a new company called Honda Motor Co. Ltd in September 1948.

Honda had been working flat-out on a new machine, with the first prototype completed in August 1949; this machine was a 98cc air-cooled two-stroke with a two-speed gearbox, and the bike produced a modest 3 bhp. The frame was a new pressed steel unit, which was extremely strong. This bike was to be called the D-type. The road trials of the new machine went so well that Honda, along with his twenty employees, celebrated their success with *doburoku* – rough, strong sake. During the party atmosphere, it was decided that just a letter for the new machine wasn't good enough so they had to come up with a name. Silence prevailed, and suddenly one of his employees shouted, 'This is like a dream!'

'That's it!' exclaimed Honda. 'We shall call it the Dream.'

While Honda himself was a good engineer, marketing and distribution was not one of his strong points. In October 1949, while on a trip to Tokyo to find an investor, Honda was fortunate enough to meet Takeo Fujisawa, who was a marketing genius; this man would become Honda's 'alter ego' and push the company forward. It wasn't long before Takeo Fujisawa got to work to sort out Honda's ad hoc distribution system, but at the same time urged Soichiro to design and build a new machine as sales of the 'Dream' were not good enough, suggesting that the new machine should have a four-stroke engine because they have a more pleasant sound. A young graduate engineer called Kiyoshi Kawashima, who had come to Honda seeking a job back in 1948, helped Soichiro Honda design a new 146cc four-stroke engine. In recognition of his contribution to the Dream E-type, Honda later made Kawashima a director of the company – he was only thirty-four. By 1950 Honda had established an office in Tokyo and made Takeo Fujisawa Director in Charge of Sales,

The 'Dream', a 1953 E-type – an exhibit in David Silver's museum.

and more motorcycles were being developed, such as the Dream E-type and Cub F-type. With the marketing in place in Japan and sales of machines growing, Honda and Fujisawa sought expansion overseas; armed with about £50,000, both men set off to the USA to purchase advanced machine tools that were needed for effective mass production.

By the end of 1953, the expansion program was running into difficulties; the Japanese economy was again sliding into recession, and Honda had desperate cash flow problems and was finding it difficult to pay for machines he'd bought from the USA. He decided to turn to his bank for help. Mitsubishi Bank recognised the enormous potential of Honda's export dreams so they decided to back him; his employees had the same faith and worked without bonuses or holidays. Despite all of Honda's problems at home, he was still determined to bring the export dreams to fruition. So, what was the best way to do it? 'Go racing!' he exclaimed. So, in March 1954, Honda entered a works-prepared Dream in a race in Brazil, only to finish thirteenth out of twenty-two riders. This whetted Honda's appetite for racing and he promptly announced that the company would compete in the 1959 Isle of Man TT races. Unfortunately, success was not to be, but on returning the following year Honda's riders did manage to get some points in both the 250cc and 125cc classes. Then, in 1961, Britain's own Mike Hailwood won both the 250cc and 125cc classes for Honda, putting them firmly on the world stage.

In 1959 Honda established an American subsidiary, American Honda Motor Co. Inc., which initially ordered 96 bikes, but this soon increased to 140 units a month. By 1962, having sold over 65,000 motorcycles to American buyers, Honda set up a facility in Belgium to assemble and sell mopeds in Europe. The next target for Honda was the UK, with its own large motorcycle industry; but whereas the UK mainly produced large capacity motorcycles, Honda saw an opening for much smaller everyday machines. So, in 1965, Honda UK Ltd was established. The turning point for Honda was the release in 1969 of the first real 'Superbike' – the CB750, which had a high revving 736cc in-line four-cylinder, single overhead camshaft engine, but its dominance didn't last long as Kawasaki launched a challenger in 1972 in the form of the 903cc Z1. This was the start of the death knell for the British motorcycle industry, with Honda UK capturing fifty per

A 1960s Honda RC145 race bike.

The CB750 that made a big splash in 1969 – an exhibit in David Silver's museum.

cent of the total British market. The thing with Japanese machines was that they were both more reliable and didn't leak oil. By this time, Honda was also producing motor cars and power products, such as general-purpose engines, tillers, and outboard motors.

Honda's achievements over the first twenty-five years were amazing. The company had the best engineers and Mr Honda himself was still very much hands on, but in 1973 he had been thinking about retirement. Meanwhile, Fujisawa had become tired and also wanted to retire. Mr Honda saw this as an opportunity for younger people to take the reins of his company, which was in keeping with his own philosophy that the young should be entrusted with responsibility to keep the ideas fresh and new. So, when he told the board of directors his intention, Honda himself proclaimed that both men would retire on the twenty-fifth anniversary of the company. Soichiro was the President and Takeo Fujisawa was Executive Vice President, so in September 1973 both men officially retired, but the board of directors gave them each the title of Director and Supreme Advisor. Kiyoshi Kawashima succeeded Soichiro Honda as President.

# 2

# The Concept

The 'Spirit of the Phoenix' project, which Honda was working on, created some of the new custom-style motorcycles in the early '80s through to the '90s, starting with the Magna series – V-twin and V4-engined machines – followed by the Steed and Shadow series V-twins, along with the retro-styled 'American Classic Edition' (which Honda referred to as a 'Radical Custom'), and a new cruiser that would become the pinnacle of the range of Honda Custom machines. This machine would be known as the 'Valkyrie' in North America, Canada, Australia and Japan, but in Europe only would be known as the 'F6C'. The Spirit of the Phoenix project was, 'The Blaze of Freedom... Honda's Customs promise a full-throttle, wide-open ride to the horizon. Created in the robust spirit of motorcycles born of the American landscape'. This was the theme of the 'Custom Section' on the Honda stand at the thirtieth Tokyo Motor Show held in 1993.

The Valkyrie project started life in 1991 with a single design sketch by a senior designer at the Honda Technical Research Institute, Asaka, in Japan; his name was Mr Kitagawa. He also worked closely with Honda Research & Development Americas (HRA) on this project, especially with Joe Boyd, an American Honda engineer, to get the full American feel for this new machine. His sketches portrayed a performance cruiser with a strong Honda identity. A slightly different concept to the fashion of the time, one design was based more on the VF750 Magna of the early '80s; Mr Kitagawa felt that the engine in the GL1500 Gold Wing would be the ideal platform for this project, as that is what the Spirit of the Phoenix project was about, the sense of presence and power, along with the basic form of low seat and teardrop fuel tank. His thoughts were that this engine had been under cover far too long and he wanted to make the opposed-six-cylinder engine the focal point for this new cruiser. The first early sketch depicted the bike with fuel tank flowing into the seat, with side cowls for dispersing heat from the radiators sitting on top of each bank of cylinders.

An air-dam fitted under the front of the engine flowed into the short exhaust system and the front forks were huge inverted type. The bike's ground clearance looked high, but the seat height was low; the seat itself was drawn as a complete unit and included a passenger backrest. The rear fender was 'bobber'-like and incorporated the rear light unit; the bike's name on the fuel tank was 'Diablo'. One interesting part of the design was the fork-like swingarm, which would incorporate a revolutionary hydraulic drive system.

One of the original drawings for the Valkyrie project. (Honda)

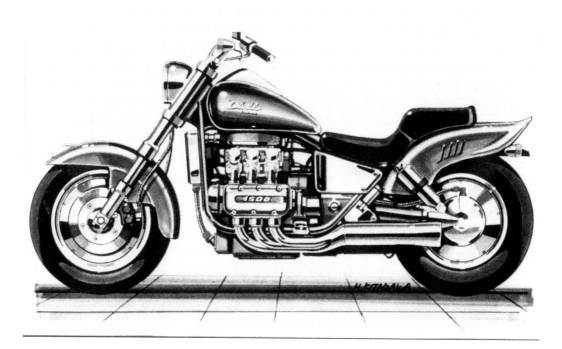

This drawing shows more of the engine and the carburettors. (Honda)

The ìretroî style, showing more flowing lines. (Honda)

The new cruiser in clay mock-up form. (Honda)

A later drawing in 1992 showed the bike with more of the engine visible, with six carburettors – three each side – and the teardrop fuel tank stopping just short of the seat. This version had two three-into-one megaphone-style exhausts and the rear suspension was dual, with sharply raked shock absorbers. From the lower part of the engine (water-pump housing) to the bottom of the radiator, the drawing shows a steel braided long water hose and the rear fender was still a 'bobber' style. A few other sketches emerged to establish the direction this new custom cruiser would take.

One other drawing the press and public got to see showed a totally different direction for the bike, with its ìretroî style and deep mudguards; it now had a longer wheelbase and more flowing lines, and the engine design was near to how the finished article would look. The exhaust was much longer with three down-pipes flowing into a straight muffler. This design emerged as the favoured one by both the Japanese design team and American Honda, who saw the design as 'Classic American' with its 1950s styling and features and aggressive-looking six-cylinder engine.

Next came the clay model. The engine looked finished in every detail and the exhaust system from the previous drawing was much longer with fish-tail ends. The engineers fitted rear passenger floorboards, with the rear seat just a small pad type; they also kept the inverted long front forks from the earlier drawings. This clay mock-up did actually become a finished working bike.

In April 1994, American Honda surprised the press and public by arranging with a motorcycle accessories shop – Accessories Unlimited in Valencia, California – to put on

The prototype featured in MCN in 1994. (Art Friedman)

15

# First pictures of top-secret classic-styled retro low-rider with 1500cc GoldWing power

**BY ADAM SMALLMAN**
**PICTURES ART FRIEDMAN**

THESE are exclusive first pictures of an all-new six-cylinder Honda custom cruiser that is set to steal sales from Harley-Davidson in the massive U.S. retro market.

The new bike - likely to be called a NightWing or WideWing - uses the giant 100bhp flat-six motor currently used in Honda's GL1500 GoldWing super-tourer.

The pictures, taken at top-secret road trials near Los Angeles, California, show Honda has unashamedly lifted the bike's styling from classic American machines of the past.

Two-tone paintwork, long, straight, low-slung exhausts, giant Indian-style fenders and heavy, wide-set forks give the machine a muscular, spartan low-rider look.

And the WideWing's disc wheels (17-inch front and 15-inch rear) are a blatant copy of those on Harley's big-selling Fat Boy.

Acres of obligatory chrome-plating adorn the engine casings, rear shocks, shaft drive, headlamp and instruments.

The bike retains the GoldWing's five-speed gearbox, but the GL1500's reverse gear - needed to manoeuvre the massive 810lb, fully-faired tourer - has been ditched.

Riders invited to the secret tests report massive torque on the machine - likely to be identical to the Wing's 110ftlb at 4000rpm, but offering far superior

acceleration because of the new bike's substantially lower weight.

The WideWing was created by Honda in Japan but will be market-tested in the U.S.

A Honda UK spokesman said he was unaware of the new bike, but added it would be unlikely to come to Britain before 1995.

**■ RETRO SPEC: Indian-type fenders add to classic look**

## 'Giant Indian-style fenders and wide-set forks give it a spartan, muscular look'

**■ SIX TOY: Heavily chromed six-cylinder GoldWing engine makes 100bhp and 110ftlb**

One day the world would get to ride the production version. The article in MCN was written by Adam Smallman, with Art Friedman supplying the pictures.

a display of new concept custom bikes just to get the public's feeling regarding their designs. On show were a radical 750 Magna, along with the nameless horizontally opposed six-cylinder-engined cruiser. American Honda and Honda Research of America employees were on hand to get feedback for the exercise. Onlookers were told by Honda representatives that the 'GL-based cruiser was just a concept vehicle' and that 'the get-together was primarily to conduct research on the overall custom-bike market', but Art Friedman, the senior editor of the American magazine *Motorcyclist*, said in his report on the bike that the machine was too close to a production unit, stating that 'judging by the integrated look and overall quality of the flat-six machine, we'd bet money the bike is well past the prototype stage and probably being readied for production, possibly with an introduction date as early as 1995'. Another American motorcycle magazine, *Rider*, referred to the new 'Six' as a 'Harley-on-steroids-styled machine'. Editor Mark Tuttle Jr was told that the engine was the same 1,520cc stock unit as the Gold Wing but the chassis and running gear were all one-off components, although the differential certainly looked like a Gold Wing unit.

Mr Kitagawa achieved his aim of making the six-cylinder engine dominate the total bike; this huge fully chromed engine gleamed in the sunlight, the wheels were semi-disc like, with a reported 17-inch front and a 15-inch rear both carrying wide fat tyres. In *Motor Cycle News (MCN)*, 27 April 1994, Adam Smallman commented that the wheels were a 'blatant copy of those on Harley's big-selling Fat Boy'. The frame was new and nothing like the one used on the Gold Wing, although the swingarm and rear calliper carrier looked, again, like a Gold Wing unit. The single headlight appeared to just be stuck between the highly polished forks and the top and bottom fork-yokes. The instruments (a speedometer and tachometer), along with the front indicators, were mounted to the very wide handlebars. Steel braided hoses were fitted to the top and bottom of the radiator and the front engine guards had some sort of radiator protection integrated into them with chrome front covers.

A single chrome-covered horn was fitted on the left-hand side between the radiator and fuel tank. The large teardrop fuel tank did actually carry fuel as opposed to the Gold Wing's setup of fuel tank under the seat. Just below the tank, on the left, was the ignition switch. The mudguards were large and swept; the rear carried a VT600 Shadow-style rear light unit, while the rear indicators were mounted to the chrome trims that fixed to the sides of the mudguard. Braking was carried out using triple discs with twin-piston callipers; the front discs looked similar to the ones fitted to Honda's CB500. Passenger comfort seemed meagre with just a small individual seat pad, while the rider got a long, wide seat; Honda did, however, fit some very nice chrome-plated rear passenger floorboards. Speculation regarding a name for the new bike by some onlookers included 'Night Wing' and 'Wide Wing', but no actual name badges were on the bike except for a pair of large chrome Honda emblems fitted to the fuel tank.

Released in 1985, the Yamaha V-Max with its 1,197cc, 70 degree V-Four engine and 'Muscle bike' looks.

# 3

# Power Cruisers

## 1997 GL1500 C-V and GL1500 CT-V Tourer (MZ0)

Joe Boyd, a Honda engineer nicknamed 'GL Joe' due to his love of Gold Wings, was considered the driving force behind the Valkyrie as he really believed in the project. So, after five years of development, American Honda finally launched its new cruiser, which had been shown to the public as a prototype a couple of years earlier. The flat-six Valkyrie (designated GL1500C) was shown at the Rosemont Convention Centre on 19 January 1996. Honda unveiled the monster cruiser as an early 1997 model, full production started on 11 April 1996 at American Honda's facility in Marysville, Ohio, with seventy units programed to be built on the first day.

Everybody thought the horizontally opposed 1,520cc six-cylinder engine, which had a bore and stroke of 71 x 64 mm (2.8 x 2.5 inches), was essentially the same unit Honda used in the Gold Wing, but it wasn't. The only thing they had in common was the bore and stroke and the fact that they were both horizontally opposed six-cylinder engines; as complete engines, they don't even look the same. The Valkyrie's cylinder blocks had solid engine mounts (as the engine is a stress-member); the Gold Wings' were rubber-mounted. The tachometer red-line limit was higher by 1,000 rpm over the Gold Wings', while the Valkyrie red-lined at 6,500 rpm. To boost the engine power of the Valkyrie up to 106 bhp at 6,000 rpm, Honda decided to do away with the hydraulic tappets of the Gold Wing and instead used screw/nut tappets that needed inspecting or adjusting every 12,000 miles. The single overhead camshafts were redesigned along with the valves and were operated via two rubber inverted toothed belts, covered by a one-piece full width, chrome cam-belt cover. Honda used the same crankshaft as in the Gold Wing's engine but modified the pistons and ring sets; the transmission cover was also modified to cater for the new water pump, and the five-speed gearbox used different gear ratios, which was operated via a hydraulic clutch. The rear case had the orifice capped off where the Gold Wing's reverse-gear mechanism fitted, as the Valkyrie didn't have that luxury. Engine cooling was via a large single radiator, cooled with a single fan. The radiator was mounted behind the front wheel just above the timing belt cover (which made timing belt inspection easier). Honda neatly tucked the cooling reservoir under the left-hand side cover, the system held

The author taking a US-spec GL1500 Valkyrie for a test ride at the Gold Wing Owners Club Treffen at Detling in 1996. Honda UK brought in a couple of these bikes for promotion. (Wendy Rakestrow)

0.825 imperial gallons (3.75 litres) of coolant, less than the Gold Wing's much larger cooling system. The dry weight of the Valkyrie was 681 lbs (309 kg), with the engine weighing in at 262 lbs (118.7 kg), just over thirty-eight per cent of the bike's total dry weight. Six 28-mm Constant Velocity diaphragm-type carburettors fed the engine with fuel, while the large airbox helped it breathe; Honda put a nice touch on top of the airbox lid, 'F6', but unfortunately it was only visible when removing the fuel tank. The fuel tank was mounted in the conventional place as opposed to the Gold Wing's under seat unit, the tank held 4.4 imperial gallons (20 litres, 5.3 US gallons). Looking at a side shot of the Valkyrie's engine, it does look like a GL1200 Gold Wing on steroids, with two extra cylinders, the out-of-the-frame sloping carburettors, along with the separate inlet manifolds. The frame is made up of thirty-one different parts, construction is a 'Diamond' type with the two front down-tubes mounting directly to the top of the engine; at the swingarm pivot-point there are two large castings on either side welded to the tubular steel frame and two separate sub-frames run along the bottom side of the engine. To give the bike more of a custom look, Honda raked the forks at 32.2 degrees with a trail of 152 mm (6 inches). The front Showa fork legs were an unusual application for a cruiser, more in keeping with sports bikes. The long, inverted type (similar to the early prototype bike) gave the forks more rigidity and, having a stanchion diameter of 45 mm, fork travel was 130 mm (5.1 inches).

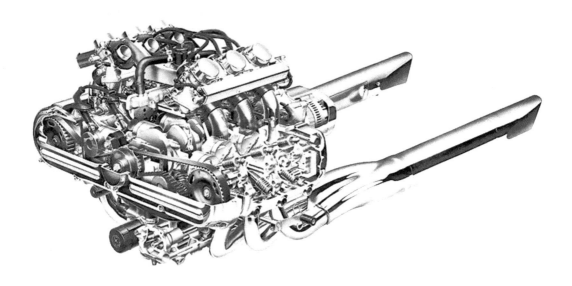

*Above*: The horizontally opposed six-cylinder engine – the heart of the Valkyrie. (Honda)

*Left*: The F6C's impressive power plant, awash with chrome plating as standard; note three of its six carburettors.

The Valkyrie/F6C's starter motor under the right-hand side cover, bolted to the back of the GL1500 engine.

The other three carburettors, along with the ignition switch on the right-hand side of the bike.

The five-way adjustable rear shock absorbers, a special tool for adjustment is in the tool-kit.

The new forks had chrome covers fitted to protect the stanchions and seals. At the rear, there were two fully chromed shock absorbers with five-position manual adjustment for dampening; rear travel was 120 mm (4.7 inches). Honda managed to keep the wheelbase of the Valkyrie the same as the Gold Wing at the time – a long 1,690 mm (66.5 inches). The rear engine case and the swingarm, although modified parts, were similar to that of the Gold Wing; Honda redesigned the rubber boot that covered the universal joint on the Valkyrie that went from the engine case to the swingarm, making it cone shaped and giving it much more clearance between the boot and universal joint. The one fitted to the GL1500 Gold Wing was straight and over a period of time the universal joint would wear a hole in the rubber boot, which could lead to premature universal joint failure. The funny thing was that the two motorcycles were built in the same factory on the same production line yet Honda never fitted the modified boot to the Gold Wing. The exhaust system of the Valkyrie was very long and sleek but hid the fact that it was a free-flowing six-into-six system. A muffler each side contained straight through pipes, which could be seen in the vertical semi 'fin'-looking tailpipe. The ignition switch wasn't in the conventional place up on the headstock, but mounted on the right-hand side below the fuel tank and the choke was located in the left-hand switchgear. On starting the Valkyrie, it gave a mighty growl through the long silencers – a real 'Hot Rod' sound.

The nice, clean, easy to read speedometer and tachometer. Note the three information lights in the headlamp shell.

The Valkyrie emblem fitted to the USA, Canadian, Australian and Japanese models.

The 'Spirit of the Phoenix', part of the F6C's emblem.

The new Valkyrie emblem first fitted to the Interstate model in 1999.

The clean design of the final drive unit. On later models Honda polished the housing.

Braking on the Valkyrie was conventional, with twin-piston hydraulic callipers at the front clamping to twin 296 mm full-floating discs. These are designed in a way to let the disc expand as heat builds up, but still maintain braking torque to the carrier. The rear was a single 316 mm disc, again with a twin-piston hydraulic calliper. All the discs had a hole configuration in them that helped disperse heat and stop brake fade. On the Valkyrie, Honda used matching wheels, each having three pairs of blade-like spokes – the front being 3.5 inches wide, carrying a 150/80-HR17 radial tyre, while the rear was a massive 5-inch-wide wheel carrying a 180/70-HR16 radial. The rear's diameter was an inch bigger than the one reported to be on the 'prototype' back in 1994. The front mudguard was a lot larger than the prototype's, covering more of the side of the tyre and wheel with the paintwork, especially on the two-tone colours, giving the mudguards a shouldered look. Honda also added a subtle centre crease on each guard. The totally new frame and the fact the fuel tank was in the conventional place allowed Honda engineers the chance to give the Valkyrie a low seat height, at just 29.1 inches (739 mm), although this was not low by custom bikes standards, the lowest at the time being Harley's Fat Boy, with a very low 25.8 inches (655 mm). The way the Valkyrie's seat itself was designed gave a real overall custom feel. The seat was made in two halves complete with passenger backrest as standard and as the bike was more of a 'Hot Rod' cruiser rather than a conventional one, by removing the passenger seat and backrest the owner could give the bike a 'Hot Rod' look. The front section of the seat didn't require any tools for its removal, just the ignition key. The location of the seat lock was just below the fuel tap on the left-hand side; by removing the seat the battery could be accessed, along with the tool kit and owner's manual. Although with the Valkyrie, the passenger accommodation seemed better with the backrest compared to the prototype bike, Honda didn't fit the rear floorboards to the production model; instead, they used the foot pegs from the VT1100C. As the Valkyrie was built at the Marysville factory in Ohio by Honda of America Manufacturing (HAM), and they were so proud of this fact, they printed 'Made in USA' on the rear of the passenger seat below the Honda name.

Front engine guards were standard, following the lines of the chrome cam-belt cover, and a single horn was mounted on the right beside the radiator, which did look like an afterthought. On the prototype bike, the instruments and front indicators were mounted on the handlebars but Honda decided to move them for production, fixing bullet-shaped speedometer and tachometer with easy-to-read white-coloured faces to the top yoke. The instruments were hinged, thus allowing for slight angle adjustment. The tachometer had three warning lights fitted – engine temperature, oil and side stand – while the other three were in the headlight shell: neutral light, indicators and main beam. The headlight was a clear reflector type with a unique built-in visor. Although the rear indicators were mounted to the prototype's chrome rear mudguard trims, Honda decided to move them to the number-plate bracket on the production model, just below the single rear light. This certainly was destined to be a motorcycle the after-market accessories companies would go mad with; the bike was already loaded with chrome, but they would just make more!

Honda themselves made a lot of accessories for the Valkyrie, ranging from exhaust tips to a handlebar-mounted CB radio. They knew customers would want to fit more electrical gadgets, so accommodated them by fitting a 5-amp accessory terminal under the right-hand side cover. The whole electrical system was powered by a 20AH battery and charged with a 546-watt alternator. As with other motorcycles in their range, Honda fitted a bank-angle sensor for safety, located just behind the seat-lock panel. This would kill the engine if the bike fell over with the engine running.

Honda was aware that calling the bike a Valkyrie in Europe probably wasn't a good idea as it might offend some people, so chose to call the bike an 'F6C' ('Flat-Six Custom') instead; the fuel tank emblems reflected that. In the USA, Canada, Australia and Japan the bike was known as a 'Valkyrie'; the fuel tank emblem referenced this as well as the fact it was a Flat-6. Some European riders, however, didn't like that Honda chose to call the bike an 'F6C' and so changed the emblems.

So, why was it called a Valkyrie? Normally cruisers are laid-back, feet forward machines, but not this one; Honda described it by saying, 'The Valkyrie is poised to take on its role as the baddest bike on the boulevard'. Where does the name 'Valkyrie' come from? It's Norse mythology, referring to the god Odin and his twelve handmaidens who were called 'Valkyries'. According to the myth, when a Viking was slain in battle a warrior maiden (Valkyrie) would choose half of the slain and escort them to Valhalla, which was the heavenly abode of Odin's army.

In the States, the Valkyrie was offered in four colours, three of which were two-tone; American Red with Pearl Glacier White, black with the aptly-named Pearl Hot Rod Yellow, Pearl Majestic Purple with Pearl Glacier White, and, lastly, solid black. Modern Honda

*Above*: The coolant reservoir tank under the left-hand side cover. On the frame tube is the bike's colour label.

*Left*: The front and rear photographs of this F6C belie the full width of the bike.

In November 1996 American Honda issued a recall notice regarding the rear indicator mounts. This only affected a small amount of production.

The top radiator hose along with the radiator filler cap. Note the frame number plate, this is on the right on the UK F6C and on the left on the US-specification Valkyrie.

The bottom radiator hose was long and a bit unsightly. Note the oil filter to the left of the water-pump housing.

motorcycles always come with a colour label stating the model and colour code for the bike; on the Valkyrie/F6C this was located under the left-hand side cover, stuck to the frame.

The UK launch of the GL1500 Valkyrie was at the London Motorcycle Show at Adrenalin Village, Chelsea Bridge, on 15 June 1996; Honda UK imported two of the American-built Valkyries for the public to view at the show. Later in the year, Honda UK displayed a European specification F6C at the International Motorcycle Show at the N.E.C, Birmingham. Although the most obvious difference between the American and European models was the fuel tank emblems, underneath Honda had executed major changes; a couple of gear ratios were changed, the secondary reduction and fourth gear, and the exhaust was not so free-flowing as the American unit – in the end of the tailpipe the Valkyrie/F6C's had three small pipes; the American models are much larger (22 mm) than the European ones (15 mm). In 1991 the European Commission had proposed a 100 brake horsepower (bhp) limit for motorcycles, which the manufacturers adhere to (though France is the only country that enforced it). The upshot to this was the F6C had slightly reduced power over its American counterpart; Honda achieved this by altering the camshafts and timing, together with modest re-jetting of the main jet in the carburettors, which brought the bhp down to the limit of 100.

The exhaust tail end on the F6C and Valkyrie have different sized triple pipes. The F6C's are 15 mm (as shown) while the Valkyrie's are a larger 22 mm. Most owners seem to cut them out to give the bike a different exhaust tone.

A 1998 'Blaze Yellow and Cream' Valkyrie in standard condition, which is very hard to find.

Other changes were to the headlight. The 7-inch unit was altered to a standard glass type, as opposed to the American model's clear plastic reflector unit, but it still featured the visor. US motorcycles compulsorily come with side front and rear reflectors, the European models don't but the F6C had a black blank on each side of the radiator and no rear ones at all. The mirrors were round, while the American models used rectangular-shaped ones. With weather conditions around the world being somewhat different, Honda clear-coat lacquered the wheels on the European models for protection against the elements. Although Honda called the American, Canadian, Australian and Japanese models 'Valkyrie', and they were part of The Spirit of the Phoenix project, it was only the F6C's fuel tank emblem that had an association with the project; Honda incorporated the 'Phoenix' emblem within the F6C's emblem. Two colour options were available to the UK market – American Red with Pearl Glacier White and solid black.

In the USA, the Valkyrie was available from 25 May 1996, but before this American Honda went to great lengths to publicise this new cruiser with a magazine, TV, and point-of-sale ad campaign, which were designed to tease potential customers. The adverts would only show partial images of the new cruiser, and said 'you'll have to wait until the big day'. The Valkyrie's price was set at $12,499 for the solid black and $12,799 for the two-tone colours, but could have sold for a lot more as demand at American Honda dealers was high, with a Honda spokesman telling the *Columbus Dispatch* newspaper that the first six months of production had already sold out. In the UK, the F6C wasn't available until January 1997. For both colours, Honda UK set the price at £11,950.

Since it was first shown as a prototype back in 1994, motorcycle publications in both America and Britain had been very enthusiastic about this new cruiser Honda was working on. The March 1996 issue of *Cycle World* (a US publication) featured the Valkyrie, with Matthew Miles doing a four-page article; on the contents page, he said this was 'not your

The Valkyrie Tourer in black with Pearl Twilight Silver. In certain light the silver had a pink hue.

The large 4.4 imperial gallon (20 litre) fuel tank and simplistic instruments.

*Left*: The Valkyrie Tourer's hard panniers; note the unpleasant seam running down the back of them.

*Below*: The one rear lock that opens the 35-litre pannier. On the top left of the lid there is a small handle for opening. This photo shows an inner bag, but they weren't standard equipment.

father's Gold Wing' – and he was right, it wasn't a Gold Wing at all! The front cover shot was the best of any magazine's coverage with a pull-out double page spread of the side of the bike from the front. Brian Blades took the studio pictures of an American Red and Pearl Glacier White Valkyrie – a beautiful elevated shot featured in the article. Bill Wood was the journalist who witnessed the first Valkyrie to be built on a production line; as managing editor for *American Motorcyclist* magazine Bill was invited by Honda America Manufacturing (HAM) to partake in the manufacturing process. Asked which colour he would choose, he replied 'I'd be happy to take whatever they were building, but a black-and-yellow bumblebee model sure looked nice'. The beginning of the production line tour started at 9 a.m. and at 12.18 p.m. Bill rode the 'bumblebee' off the production line. The interesting thing with the first Valkyrie off the line was it doesn't appear to have any pin-striping on the paintwork. British publications got their hands on the Valkyrie too, with *Bike* magazine's July 1996 issue reporting on the world launch of the bike in California, where journalist Andy Saunders got to ride a pre-production unit. He seemed impressed. *Motorcycle Sport and Leisure* magazine, July 1996 issue, included a two-page short article on the Honda UK Valkyrie test bike; again, their journalist '*The Spy*' was also impressed and said, 'Unquestionably the Valkyrie lives up to its name with 'out of this world' looks and performance. But don't buy one if you wish to remain anonymous or dislike polishing chrome!' Monstrous great bikes are normally frowned upon by the press, especially the British press, because they are generally not fast, don't handle well and, in their opinion, are rubbish, but the Valkyrie/F6C was different; it was huge, handled well with its radial tyres, was pretty quick off the mark and it even wheelied! Five stars to Honda then.

In America, Honda's advertising campaign got well underway with a three-page spread in the July 1996 issue of *Motorcyclist* magazine; this coincided with the magazine doing their first Valkyrie road test. The advert for the Valkyrie headlined 'THE FAT LADY HAS SUNG', with a nice shot of the chromed engine. Over the page Honda used the headline 'INTRODUCING THE VALKYRIE'; the Valkyrie they used for the shot was a black and Pearl

The two-tone paintwork giving the front mudguard a shouldered look, while the 17-inch front wheel carries a large 150-80/R17 radial tyre.

Hot Rod Yellow bike; interestingly this bike had a silver pinstripe and not the production orange. *Motorcyclist* carried out a comprehensive road test and even managed to show all three two-tone colours of the bike on offer; they remarked that 'you probably won't threaten many sportbike riders on the Valkyrie, but a good rider might be able to make a few question their religion'. They also commented on the Valkyrie's amazing torque that impressed them with 96.1 foot-pounds being produced between 4,250 to 4,500 rpm – a new record from a production motorcycle. In a side bar article entitled 'Full Circle', *Motorcyclist* talked about the Valkyrie's roots and Honda's original engineering concept, the M1, along with the GL1000 Gold Wing being similar all those years ago. The following month's issue of *Motorcyclist* featured their annual 'The Best of Motorcycling'. Out of nineteen categories Honda won seven and drew one; 'Best Open Cruiser' award went to the new Valkyrie as it wasn't a normal styled cruiser with 'that' engine.

*Motorcycle Cruiser* was a brand-new quarterly sister magazine to *Motorcyclist*, which featured the Valkyrie in its 'Premier Issue', spring 1996. The headline read: 'Honda Valkyrie, Gold Wing with an attitude'. They said that the Valkyrie doesn't fit the same mould as your run-of-the-mill cruiser, mainly because of the engine. They also said, 'Others will recognise exactly the machine they have been waiting for in this mould-smashing motorcycle'. In their third issue, *Motorcycle Cruiser* pointed out some of the Valkyrie's failings, saying that the seat height was tall for a cruiser and the engine design makes foot-peg positioning

The Tourer was first sold as a 1997 model, but not in the UK.

*Right*: The left-hand switchgear and hydraulic clutch fluid reservoir, with the choke incorporated into the switchgear housing.

*Below*: The right-hand switchgear with starter, engine kill and light switches from a UK model. All switchgear was polished cast aluminium.

*Above*: The Valkyrie was built in America and they were proud of the fact.

*Left*: The passenger accommodation was minimal, although the backrest was a standard feature.

The Valkyrie Tourer emblem fitted to the side of pannier. For the 1998 model Honda fitted one to the windscreen as well.

limited. Some quality issues came up too, including the rust-prone and ugly passenger foot-peg brackets and the unsightly lower radiator hose, which just hangs there! In their opinion, with all the chrome, the black horn was a bit misplaced and also not very effective, being 'inoffensive to the ear'. The other thing on this stunning machine, with its fully chromed engine, was the appearance of the rear engine mounts, which had a dull matt finish and again were prone to corrosion. In a later edition of the magazine they also did a feature entitled 'Best of Cruising' in which they asked readers to vote for the 'Best of' in twelve different cruising categories – five for the actual bikes and seven for associated items. The Valkyrie was voted 'Best New-for-1997 Cruiser'.

Roger Lambert, senior manager of company communications at HAM, said the Valkyrie was being marketed at three different groups of people: 'current Gold Wing owners as an additional motorcycle, baby boomers who were returning to motorcycling and custom bike owners who were looking to change motorcycles and move-up to a more performance cruiser'.

So, what was the Valkyrie's competition? Living with convention, or not in the Valkyrie's case, bikes with powerful Cruiser engines didn't exist until Honda produced this (with the Yamaha V-Max as the exception), mainly because the engine of choice with Cruisers (as far as the manufacturers were concerned) was a mildly tuned V-twin.

In a magazine buyers' guide for 1997, Harley-Davidson had seventeen Cruiser models to choose from while both Honda and Kawasaki had six. Suzuki had three with its Intruder and Marauder series and Yamaha also offered six. All of these bike's engines were V-twins. Yamaha did offer the most with a V-four engine with their Royale Star and V-Max range.

European models of the F6C used a standard glass headlamp.

Valkyrie models had a clear reflector type unit.

The Valkyrie Tourer's windshield that wrapped around the headlight and shaped around the indicators. Later models had a 'Tourer' emblem fitted.

At the American Honda Dealer convention on 24 October 1996, Honda announced that they would be releasing a 'Tourer' version of the Valkyrie, which would be available to dealers as of 15 January 1997. The Tourer came complete with colour-matched 35-litre hard-shell panniers (with new Tourer emblems), which incorporated rear protection bars into the mounts. The panniers featured a single lock at the rear of each one with the lid hinged at the front and opening from the rear; a neat little moulded handle helped assist with the opening and the lid was tethered to the base via a cable. Each pannier could hold a maximum load of 20 lbs (9 kg) of luggage. At the front, Honda fitted a large Lexan windshield that wrapped around the headlamp and curved around the front indicators; this came with nicely shaped chrome-plated mounting hardware. Three colour combinations were offered for the GL1500CT Valkyrie Tourer – American Red with Pearl Glacier White, Pearl Sonoma Green with Pearl Ivory Cream, and the bike was also available in solid black. The price for the Valkyrie Tourer was $14,499 for the two-tone colours and $13,999 for the solid black.

In the States, sales of the Valkyrie were going quite nicely, and then the arguments started; the Valkyrie is a naked Gold Wing; therefore, it should be allowed in the Gold Wing clubs – hang-on, the Valkyrie isn't a Gold Wing, it's a Valkyrie or F6C. But it has a Gold Wing engine? No, it doesn't, it has an engine that is similar to the one used in a Gold Wing. But could you put a Valkyrie's engine with its carburettors into a Gold Wings frame? No, it won't fit; there would be no room for the six carburettors anyway so what is the point?

Some Gold Wing clubs and organisations around the world did allow the Valkyrie owners to join. In America, the Gold Wing Road Riders Association (GWRRA) was one of them, stating on the cover of March 2000's *Wing World* magazine that the organisation was 'for the Gold Wing and Valkyrie rider'. The cover for that month featured a black and Pearl Hot Rod Yellow Valkyrie in a petrol station on the old US Route 66 in Willams, Arizona. The magazine also featured a ride on the Valkyrie Interstate. By the December 2004 issue, the sub-heading was dropped and the following month the magazine header was totally redesigned with the sub-header of 'Ultimate Luxury Motorcycle Touring'. When a member wrote to *Wing World* complaining that there never seemed to be any articles on the Valkyrie in the magazine, the answer came back – well write something!

Nowadays there are numerous well-established Valkyrie/F6C owner's clubs around the world concentrating just on that model. On 20 November 2013, Honda was to drop another bombshell to the Valkyrie/F6C and Gold Wing club world by releasing a new Valkyrie/F6C eleven years after the demise of the original GL1500 Valkyrie, but this time it *would be* a stripped-down Gold Wing – the GL1800 Gold Wing Valkyrie or F6C.

The seat lock located just under the fuel tank. To the left is the bleed valve for the hydraulic clutch.

# 1998 GL1500 C-W and GL1500 CT-W Tourer

1997 was a near-perfect year for the Valkyrie/F6C as Honda didn't feel the need to improve or change anything apart from the needle jet in the carburettors, the front wheel bearings, and obvious colour changes. One small change to the Tourer version was the addition of a 'Tourer' emblem to the Lexan windshield.

Three new two-tone colour choices were offered to the American buyers for the Valkyrie in 1998 – Pearl Sedona Red with Pearl Ivory Cream, Pearl Coronado Blue with Pearl Ivory Cream, and Blaze Yellow with Pearl Ivory Cream, with solid black still remaining an option. The Valkyrie Tourer was offered in the solid black and also two new two-tone colours – Pearl Sedona Red with Pearl Ivory Cream and black with Pearl Jade Green.

American Honda increased their prices for both the Valkyrie and Valkyrie Tourer. The increase was small; only $300, which made $12,799 for a solid black Valkyrie and $13,099 for the two-tone colours. The Tourer didn't go up as much in price; the solid black sold for $14,199, while the two-tone versions were $14,699. This represented $200 over the 1997 model.

Here in the UK, Honda was busy focusing on a competition with a trip to the USA as the prize. A custom motorcycle brochure featured the F6C as a black and white poster on one side along with other Hondas in the custom range. On the reverse side Honda offered owners a

One of the brighter colour combinations for the Valkyrie in 1998 and 1999 Blaze Yellow with Pearl Ivory Cream.

The emblem fitted to the Tourer's windscreen in 1998.

range of accessories under the heading 'Customise and Personalise your Honda Cruiser'. The brochure also included model details and specifications. To enter the competition, all riders had to do was take a test ride on any of the five Honda cruisers – the F6C, two of the Rebel or two of the Shadow series – before 1 September 1998; the trip for two was to Marysville, Ohio, courtesy of American Honda. The competition asked three simple, multiple choice questions: question one, 'Where is the Honda F6C manufactured?'; question two, 'What is the engine configuration of the F6C?'; question three, 'What is the F6C's final drive?' As you can guess all the answers are somewhere in this book! But it's too late to enter as the winner was announced on 11 September 1998; I hope they enjoyed their trip!

For 1998, Honda UK imported two two-tone colour schemes for the F6C – Pearl Coronado Blue with Pearl Ivory Cream and a Europe-only colour of Pearl Canyon Copper with black. Although, according to the price list dated 6 November 1997, Honda initially maintained the UK price for the GL1500C-W at £11,950, but on 1 October 1998 Honda UK had a pricing restructure. This was mainly due to the high number of motorcycle 'Grey Imports' at the time and so they reduced the prices of the whole Honda range calling it the 'Black and White' price list, meaning that the F6C had been reduced in price by £1,955, to £9,995.

Headlined 'Flagships', the August issue of *Motorcycle Cruiser* reported on an '8 Top Cruiser Face Off', featuring a mixture of bikes – the BMW R1200C, Harley-Davidson Heritage Springer, Kawasaki Vulcan 1500 Classic, Moto Guzzi V11 EV, Suzuki Intruder 1500 LC, Triumph Thunderbird, and Yamaha Royal Star Silverado, along with the Valkyrie Tourer. In a star rating, the Honda Valkyrie was consistent with its score, having four-and-a-half stars from each of the riders, with the conclusion that 'the Valkyrie is the King of the Cruisers'.

# 1999 GL1500 C-X and GL1500 CT-X Tourer

After two model years and no major changes, Honda decided to make some small improvements to the Valkyrie and Valkyrie Tourer for 1999, giving the bikes a much smoother ride by reviewing the rear damper springs in the rear suspension. More chrome was added to both models; a new chrome cover over the horn made its appearance much neater but still didn't improve its performance. For both the Valkyrie and Tourer models, Honda offered a new colour of black with Pearl Twilight Silver and continued the solid black. The Valkyrie also had a new colour option of black with Pearl Phoenix Orange, while Blaze Yellow with Pearl Ivory Cream continued from the year before, along with Pearl Sedona Red with Pearl Ivory Cream for the Tourer model.

For European models, manufacturers had to fine tune motorcycles for the impending 'Euro-1' legislation, which came into effect on 17 June 1999. Honda reduced the exhaust emissions for the F6C to make it compliant by installing an 'Exhaust Emission Control system', which consists of a Pulse Secondary Air Injection System (PAIR). This system introduces fresh air into the exhaust system to promote the burning of unburnt exhaust gases and turns them into relatively harmless carbon dioxide and water vapour. In Japan,

The Japanese modification to the exhaust system to meet their emission laws that came into effect in October 1999.

For 1999, the Japanese market got the Valkyrie with the reverse system fitted that was first used on the Gold Wing.

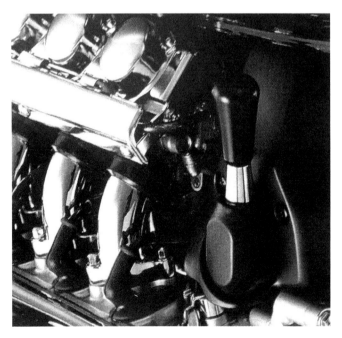

The neatly made reverse lever just behind the carburettors on the left-hand side.

This 1999 F6C model with the new horn chrome cover. The cover didn't make it sound any better.

where Honda had sold the Valkyrie since May 1996, the exhaust emission regulations that came into effect in October 1999 were even tougher.

Honda UK imported two colour options again for 1999, both two-tone – black with Pearl Twilight Silver and continued from last year with Pearl Coronado Blue with Pearl Ivory Cream as a 1999 model. Honda maintained the price for the 1999 UK-specification F6C at £9,995.

One other unique feature on the Japanese version of the Valkyrie for the 1999 model year was a reverse gear system. The system is the same as fitted to the GL1500 Gold Wing, but by installing it on the Valkyrie, Honda had to relocate the rear brake master-cylinder to a higher position. The lever for the reverse was located on the left-hand side in a vertical position; to operate the reverse gear the bike needed to be running in neutral, and the lever moved 45 degrees towards the back of the bike. Then, on pushing the starter button, the bike will move backwards at 1 mph (1.6 kph).

Exemplifying the Norse theme, Honda changed the Valkyrie and Tourer's fuel tank emblems to the same as that used on the Valkyrie Interstate, which featured a winged helmet figure. Another revised item taken from the Interstate was the bottom radiator hose protector, which replaced the unsightly one that was black steel. The Interstate's was a more tightly wound polished stainless steel version.

Honda was always looking at improving the Valkyrie's appearance, not that it really needed it, but little subtle changes make a big difference. For instance, the rear differential on the standard Valkyrie for 2000 was polished then clear-coat lacquered giving the rear a more up-market, cleaner look, although once panniers were fitted that look was no longer. The back-lamp colours of the instruments were changed as well – Honda decided to alter the colour from green to a more pleasing orange.

Even though the Valkyries were comfortable to ride – especially with the previous year's rear suspension upgrade – Honda made some changes to the seat. They reduced the seat height by 4 mm to 735 mm (28.9 inches); the front seat was slightly wider and shaped so the rider sat in it more and the passenger's section was slightly larger. The seat material finish was changed and 'Made in USA' was dropped from the rear. Honda also did a bit of weight saving by installing the tool kit from the Interstate across the Valkyrie/F6C range, which reduced the number of tools provided from seventeen items to just nine. A couple of ring spanners, Allen keys and screwdriver sets were removed.

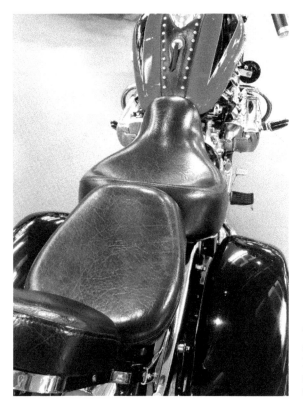

The larger seat from 2000 models onwards for the rider and passenger, Honda also changed the seat material and dropped the 'Made in USA' from the rear.

Black and yellow on this year 2000 model with silver stripe. Originally for the 1997 model, Honda were going to use this colour and stripe combination, but changed the stripe to orange for production.

For 2000 the number of colour options for both the Valkyrie and Valkyrie Tourer was reduced. The popular solid black was still on offer for both models, along with the two-tone colour black with American Red, while the standard Valkyrie also enjoyed the two-tone black with Blaze Yellow.

The F6C in Europe was still selling steadily, with Honda UK importing the 2000 models in two individual two-tone colours – the black with the Pearl Twilight Silver continued, while a new colour option of Pearl Sonoma Green Metallic with Pearl Chaparral Beige was also available as a unique colourway for European markets. Unfortunately, the lower price for the F6C didn't last that long, for the 2000 model Honda UK initially increased the price by £300 to £10,295 and then, in April, they reviewed prices across their model range, increasing the F6C to £10,499.

## 2001 GL1500 CD-1/F6C-1

After a while, mainstream publications lose interest in testing old machines. Occasionally a comparison test appears just to see if the old fuddy-duddy can still keep up with the times, but more often than not they start to fall by the wayside. Despite this, editors of *Motorcycle Cruiser* magazine in their February 2001 issue speculated that Honda would build a 1,800cc

Honda changed the paintwork on the American, Canadian and Japanese models for 2001 with a large stripe running from tip to tail. (Jacek Piterow)

version of the Valkyrie with an artist's impression of the new bike. It featured a new exhaust system, aluminium frame and redesigned side-covers and fuel tank; the magazine said it was hoping the new Valkyrie would appear as a 2003 model.

Then, in its fifth year of production, the Valkyrie/F6C was certainly going that way. Honda decided to drop the Valkyrie Tourer from the American line-up, and, in fact, from production altogether. This left the Valkyrie and Valkyrie Interstate to head the Honda Custom range. Although the Valkyrie/F6Cs weren't average cruisers with their flat-six engines, Honda decided that it was time to follow the rest instead of lead. The V-twin engine was now becoming Honda's configuration of choice for the Custom range, with the newly introduced VTX 1800. At that time, it was interesting Honda was making two different horizontally opposed six-cylinder engines. With the release of the 2001 GL1800 Gold Wing, one might have expected Honda to update the Valkyrie, but this didn't happen for the mainstream owner.

There were two small changes to the Valkyrie for the 2001 riding season and one major change that affected the bike's overall appearance. Honda gave the wheels a nice polished look, which certainly set them off with all the Valkyrie's chrome; they also changed the model designation to 'CD, Custom Deluxe' from just 'C, Custom'. The major change was to the paintwork – Honda totally changed the two-tone design, painting a three-stripe

From the 2000 model year, Honda changed the colour of the instrument lights from green to orange. (Jacek Piterow)

configuration running from the front mudguard tip, across the top of fuel tank and to the rear most tip of the rear mudguard. The three painted parts had different sized large stripes – the front mudguard at 105 mm, the fuel tank measured 135 mm, and the rear mudguard at 123 mm – all with a smaller 4 mm single stripe on each side. Three colour choices were again available: solid black, black with a Metallic Silver stripe, and Pearl Coronado Blue with a Pearl Alpine White stripe. After a short hiatus, American Honda increased the price of just the Valkyrie. Well, changes always come at a cost; the price rose to $13,099 for the solid black and $13,399 for the two-tone options.

In Britain, Honda UK increased the number of cruisers in their range by importing the new VTX1800, but also still offered the F6C. They produced a 'Custom Range' brochure for 2001 featuring the VTX1800, VT750DC, VT750C and VT125 Shadows, along with the F6C.

The European F6C, however, didn't benefit from the paintwork change as the colours on offer were a continuation from the year before – Pearl Sonoma Green Metallic with Pearl Chaparral Beige and black with Pearl Twilight Silver. Honda did manage to maintain the price at £10,499.

## 2002 GL1500 CD-2

In its penultimate year, Honda slimmed down the Valkyrie range again with the discontinuation of the Interstate model. Sales of the Honda Valkyrie were slowing down and they were becoming a hang-on-in-there machine with no real changes to the bike for years. One new colour option was the only variation for this year's model – black with an American Red stripe; the other two colours were continuations from the year before – Pearl Coronado Blue with a Pearl Alpine White Stripe and the good old solid black. For the 2002 model season, American Honda held the Valkyrie's price.

For the UK market, Honda imported the 2002 model with no changes from the previous year's bike; it didn't even come with the polished wheels of its American counterpart. This was to be the last year the F6C came to these shores in its GL1500 form as the bike was due to be discontinued worldwide. Honda UK again produced an attractive 'Custom' brochure that featured a four-page spread on the F6C along with other bikes in the range. The colour option was solid black only, which looked really nice against all that chrome. Honda again managed to maintain the price of the F6C at £10,499.

## 2003 GL1500 C/CD-3

Production of the GL1500 Valkyrie ceased in January 2003 and the final year found the bike being offered in just three countries – America, Canada and Australia. It did seem strange that American Honda would offer two versions of the Valkyrie for 2003 – one with polished wheels 'CD' (Custom Deluxe) and one without 'C' (Custom), according to the parts manual. The owner's manual also had the designation of '03 – GL1500C/CD for the US and Canadian markets. The Australian units were sold as the GL1500C-3 and they didn't have the luxury of the polished wheels. The only colour option offered in all regions was just plain old solid black.

Honda was well into the VTX programme, offering three versions of the VTX1800 and two versions of the VTX1300, which were all built at the Marysville factory in Ohio; other machines built alongside the diminishing Valkyrie were the Spirit and Sabre, two of the Shadow series. American Honda's cruiser range then consisted of one flat-six-engined machine, ten V-twins, one V-four and a vertical-twin called a 'Rebel'.

The rear mudguard of a 2001 Valkyrie with the large silver stripe on black paintwork. (Jacek Piterow)

A series of Valkyrie/F6C brochures. From the bottom left with the European 1997 F6C brochure, then through the years with the American brochures to the Valkyrie Rune brochure from Canada and lastly a 2014 Gold Wing F6C brochure from Thailand at the bottom.

Despite having only run for seven model years in three different versions, the GL1500 Valkyrie/F6C still turns heads today with its massive chrome-plated engine, huge mudguards and fat tyres. It is now difficult to find a standard Valkyrie/F6C as the bike left itself wide open to even more customising. Generally, the first thing to go was the exhaust system. Honda's decision to offer a solid black version of the Valkyrie/F6C every year was a tempting blank canvas, crying out for custom paintwork.

For the following year things started to change in the 'Cruiser' market as all the other Japanese manufacturers were churning-out V-twins by the shedload, and Harley-Davidson was also increasing their model range; this only left the British to come up with the next unusual motorcycle cruiser engine. Enter the Triumph Rocket Three, a 2,294cc (140 cubic-inch) liquid-cooled straight triple – the biggest production motorcycle engine ever. This meant the 'CC' war had come to an end with Triumph winning it hands-down, taking the crown from Honda and their 1,832cc horizontally opposed, six-cylinder engine... Honda was no longer interested.

The next generation of Valkyrie was to use the 1,832cc engine, and to most would be unaffordable, but it did still keep the Valkyrie name going for the next couple of years, until the third version appeared for the 2014 model season.

# Specifications

GL1500 Valkyrie/F6C and Valkyrie Tourer 1997–2003

Description Code
| | |
|---|---|
| Engine | SC34E |
| Frame | SC34 |

| Dimensions | Valkyrie/F6C 1997–2003 | Valkyrie Tourer 1997–2000 |
|---|---|---|
| Overall length | 2,525 mm (99.4 inches) | 2,525 mm (99.4 inches) |
| Overall width | 980 mm (38.6 inches) | 980 mm (38.6 inches) |
| Overall height | 1,185 mm (46.7 inches) | 1,485 mm (58.5 inches) |
| Wheel base | 1,690 mm (66.5 inches) | 1,690 mm (66.5 inches) |
| Ground clearance | 155 mm (6.1 inches) | 155 mm (6.1 inches) |
| Seat height '97/'99 | 739 mm (29.1 inches) | 739 mm (29.1 inches) |
| Seat height '00/'03 | 735 mm (28.9 inches) | 735 mm (28.9 inches) |

| Weight | | |
|---|---|---|
| Dry weight | 309 kg (681 lbs) | 324 kg (714 lbs) |
| | 310 kg (683 lbs) | 325 kg (716 lbs) |
| | Californian Model | Californian Model |

Engine
| | |
|---|---|
| Bore and stroke | 71.0 x 64.0 mm (2.8 x 2.5 inches) |
| Compression ratio | 9.8:1 |
| Displacement | 1,520cc (92.7 cubic-inches) |
| Carburettors | 6 x 28 mm diaphragm type CV Keihin |
| Fuel tank capacity | 20 litres (4.4 imperial gallons, 5.3 US gallons) |
| Power output | 106 bhp at 6,000 rpm (Valkyrie and Tourer) |
| | 100 bhp at 6,000 rpm (F6C) |
| | 98 bhp at 6,000 rpm (F6C, German type) |

| Power transmission | | UK Spec | US. Spec |
|---|---|---|---|
| Primary reduction | | 1.591 | 1.591 |
| Secondary reduction | | 0.939 | 0.971 |
| Gear ratio | 1st. | 2.666 | 2.666 |
| | 2nd. | 1.722 | 1.722 |
| | 3rd. | 1.291 | 1.291 |
| | 4th. | 0.964 | 1.000 |
| | 5th. | 0.805 | 0.805 |
| Final reduction | | 2.833 | 2.833 |

## Chassis and suspension

| | | |
|---|---|---|
| Castor | | 32.2 degrees |
| Trail | | 152 mm (6.0 inches) |
| Tyre size | Front | 150/80 R17 72H |
| | Rear | 180/70 R16 77H |

## Electrical

| | |
|---|---|
| Battery | 12v–20AH |
| Generator output | 546 watts |

# 4

# Reinvention of the Interstate

## 1999 GL1500 CF-X Interstate (MBY)

Giving their motorcycles a model name is something Honda has done since the company's inception. Honda's history of the Interstate name started in 1980 when the first, fully factory dressed GL1100 Gold Wing was called an 'Interstate'. The name referred to the American highways that link one state to another, which is where the Gold Wing is most comfortable. 'Interstate', as a secondary moniker, was used from 1980 to 1987 on Gold Wings and also in the mid-1980s on the 'GL' series Silver Wings, but then disappeared until 1991, with its reintroduction on the GL1500 Gold Wing Interstate. The last Gold Wing to use the Interstate name was the 1996 model, only for it to disappear again the following year.

With the introduction of a third model of Valkyrie, which went into production on 19 November 1998, Honda decided to resurrect the name again on the classic 1950s retro-styled GL1500 CF Valkyrie Interstate. This American-designed and styled Interstate was not just a standard Valkyrie with luggage and a nose-fairing, but something much more than that! With the Valkyrie Interstate, Honda wanted to move a touring machine in a different direction – the classic American way.

Due to the increased weight of the Interstate caused by adding other amenities, such as the fairing and top-box, Honda strengthened the frame by welding extra gussets below the head-stock and above the rear suspension mounts. The engine was tinkered with as well, having revised ignition timing and carburettor settings. These changes were made to give the Interstate better mid-range performance and a punchier feel. Honda also added a rubber mount to the rear of the engine to minimise vibration; the engine on the standard Valkyrie was solidly mounted. The Vehicle Description Code found within the frame and engine numbers for the Valkyrie/F6C and Valkyrie Tourer had been 'SC34'; with all the modifications Honda did to the Valkyrie Interstate, they changed the code to 'SC41'.

The front and rear suspension were uprated, again to cope with the increased loads; the spring and damping rates were revised to provide a superior ride, the rear shock absorbers still had five-position preload of adjustability and maintained the 4.7 inches (119 mm) of wheel travel, while the massive 45 mm inverted front suspension gave 5.1 inches (129 mm) of well-controlled travel. It wasn't just adding the fairing and top-box that increased the bike's weight, Honda also fitted the Interstate with a larger fuel tank than the one used on the Standard and Tourer Valkyries. The Valkyrie Interstate's fuel tank was even bigger than that of the GL1500 Gold Wing by nearly 0.5 of a US gallon, at 6.9 US gallons (26.1 litres, 5.74 imperial gallons) and 1.6 US gallons – larger than the other two bikes. Newly designed Valkyrie fuel tank emblems now featured a mythical image, which kept the Norse theme going. The Interstate's handlebars were 10 mm narrower than that of the other two Valkyries with the riders' hands sitting nicely behind the fairing for weather protection.

The Australian specification model (shown) didn't benefit from the long tail ends of the US model and has the shorter silencers of the standard model. (Steve Tyrrell)

The '50s-styled fairing with twin reflector-type headlamps. Note the clear plastic air deflectors fitted as standard.

The large rounded top-box housed the Interstate's stop/tail lamps and lock; the lever for opening the box was underneath.

The Interstate's unique lower radiator cowl.

The lower cowl incorporated air vents to cool the rider's legs in hot weather.

The front fork-mounted fairing was a retro, classical 1950s style with twin multi reflector-type headlamps, surrounded by a beautiful prominent chrome bezel. Just under the windshield was another chrome trim with a laminar-flow air-duct, which was designed to reduce low-pressure turbulence for the rider and passenger. Another air management feature was two Perspex wind-deflectors mounted at the lower part of the fairing, one on either side; these were designed to deflect air around the side of the bike. Frame-mounted cowls that acted as leg shields supplied further air management, routing hot air away from the rider's legs. Small vents were also included, and these could be opened to allow cool air to flow. As an option, Honda offered fog lights that fitted into the cowls. The fairing-mounted instruments were clean and modern with that classic look; the speedometer and tachometer had silver centres and chrome outer trims in a 1950s automotive style, and the aluminium information light panel was just below an LCD digital display, which showed riders the time, fuel level and radio/CB channels. The speedometer, although analogue, did have an electronic pick-up, along with an LCD odometer.

The Valkyrie Interstate was fitted with an AM/FM stereo radio that produced 80 watts of peak power, and for rider/passenger convenience Honda fitted an intercom communication system. The total audio package consisted of an automatic volume control and ambience setting; the normal controls were mounted on the handlebars for ease of use while riding. In all there were twelve switches for Volume Control, Tune, V-mode, Audio Mode, Band/ Memo and Speakers/Headset. The other three were Squelch, Push-to-talk and Channel Change for the optional CB radio that just plugged into the bike. The radio switch cluster featured another three buttons on the sides of the unit; a power/function button above the CB Push-to-talk button and on the other side there was a Channel Memo button below the clock function button.

Classic 1950s styling and a well thought out machine. (Steve Tyrrell)

Classic-styled instruments of the Interstate featuring modern LCD function readouts. Just above is the Laminar-flow air-duct.

Being an overall longer bike than the other two versions, Honda redesigned the mufflers and gave the Interstate longer exhaust tail ends that came level with the end of the panniers, but interestingly they turned the oval ends horizontal, giving the muffler a longer, flatter look.

The chromed rear rack carried the new rounded full-sized 'blow-moulded' 49-litre top-box, which opened via a single lock and a lever under the base. Four tail lights in two pairs were again in the traditional classic retro style and featured chrome bezels; Valkyrie was spelled out in individual chrome letters across the back of the box. Passenger comfort was very much improved with a large backrest fitted to the top-box, along with armrests; these would also accommodate the optional rear stereo speakers.

Honda also remoulded the panniers (again blow-moulded) for the Interstate; this in-turn did away with the horrible join down the back of those fitted to the Tourer. The singly locked 35-litre panniers opened at the back using the ignition key, but unlike the Tourer's, they detached via a front hook-and-catch system, with two straps in place so the lid could rest against the side of the pannier. Honda moved the location of the tool kit and owner's manual on the Interstate to the left-hand pannier; this was for convenience as they had located the main stereo unit on top of the battery box, which would have meant moving it every time access was needed to the tool kit and manual. Honda obviously didn't want riders to work on their own bikes anymore as the tool kit offered on the Interstate was very basic, with only nine tools; the important suspension adjustment tool, a flat screwdriver with separate handle, pliers, a 5-mm hexagon wrench and three spanners. With the Interstate, Honda redesigned the luggage paint scheme, which differed from that of the Tourer – it now had the two-tone colour split by the pinstripe that was shaped down and along the side of the panniers and top-box, and new Interstate emblems were fitted to the side of each pannier.

The seat fitted to the Valkyrie Interstate was a single unit as opposed to the Standard/ Tourer's dual configuration; the passenger section was much wider, which complemented the backrest. The seat itself had a firm construction and was 28.7 inches (728 mm) in height, which was 0.2 inches (6 mm) lower than that of the other two Valkyries. The Interstate's engine guards were also redesigned; now incorporating air scoops on either side just under the cylinder heads, they pushed engine and exhaust heat towards the rider's legs. With the Interstate's big, heavy look, and with its high-mounted large top-box and conventionally positioned fuel tank, the bike felt a little bit top heavy compared with the other two models. It weighed in at 774 lbs (351 kg) dry. Ground clearance was also slightly reduced to 150 mm (5.9 inches), as opposed to the Standard and Tourer's 155 mm (6.1 inches). The horn on the Interstate was repositioned and fitted to the engine guards, and the front reflectors that were either side of the radiator on the Standard and Tourer Valkyries were repositioned and mounted on the side of the front mudguard. A new unique chrome accent adorned the front mudguard, which finished the whole package off nicely. On the pre-production models, the accent read 'Valkyrie', but the wording was removed when it went into production.

Passenger armrests incorporated housings for the optional rear speakers.

Three colour options were available for the GL1500CF Valkyrie Interstate – solid black, along with two-tone colour options of either Pearl Sonoma Green Metallic with a secondary colour of Ocean Grey Metallic, or black with American Red. Prices in the USA started at $15,499 for the black unit and $15,999 for the two-tone. Honda, through its accessories division, offered Valkyrie Interstate owners twenty-four new extras for their bikes. In all, thirty-eight assorted items were available, ranging from CB radios and chrome fork covers to studded custom seats.

## 2000 GL1500 CF-Y Interstate

Only a few motorcycles were in the same class as the Interstate. The oldest was the Harley-Davidson FLH Electra Glide Classic. With its V-twin air-cooled classic engine design, its name has been around for donkey's years, but it's a design that buyers still love. Another had a V4 water-cooled engine, which from the side looked like an air-cooled twin – this being Yamaha's classically designed Royal Star Venture. In Honda's case, 'If you can't beat them then join them', but, do it a little bit differently – retro or reinvention was back! *Rider* magazine did a three-bike test in their June 1999 issue; written by Bill Stermer, its headline was 'Reinventing the Dresser.... Everything Old Is New Again'. The conclusion was that if buyers wanted a touring bike that was lighter, less complex and less expensive, any of these would do, but he thought the Yamaha offered the best overall experience and was an altogether more functional motorcycle.

Honda's marketing machine got in on the act with adverts appearing in the American press; a two-page spread showed a professional rider on a closed course, counter steering a standard Valkyrie around a bend and a series of small shots. The advert's caption read, 'Nothing can cruise like this.' Over the page was a left-hand side shot of a Valkyrie Interstate in black and American Red together with smaller pictures of its features; this time the caption was 'Nothing can tour like this.'

The hidden single lever located under the top-box.

The Interstate's unique 'Air-Scoop' welded to the underside of the engine bars.

The unique mudguard emblem on the Interstate, the pre-production units had 'Valkyrie' written on them.

1999's Interstate was built nearly perfectly, as the new model only had a few parts modified, such as the rear wheel axle, rear disc and the tail lights. One other item was the rubber strap to hold the tool kit in position, although instead of the part being the same substantial strap as the previous year (which was first used on the 1974 Honda XL350), for the 2000 model it was more like an elastic band.

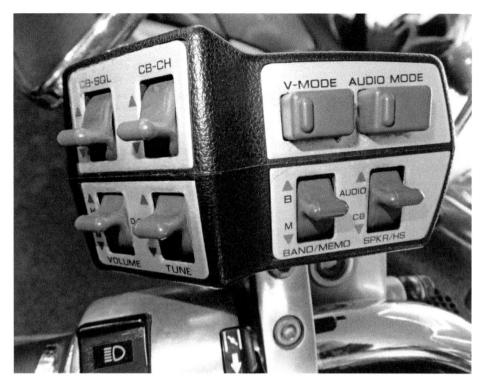

The left-hand radio/CB radio switch cluster with an array of twelve switches and buttons in total.

Three colours were offered for the 2000 model year, two continued from the previous year – solid black and black with American Red. The new colour, Pearl Coronado Blue with the secondary colour of Pearl Twilight Silver, was a really nice combination; the silver in certain light gave off a beautiful pink hue. Honda maintained its prices for the 2000 model year for the Interstate.

The Interstate was available in just three countries worldwide – America, Canada and Australia. Markets around the world differ in specification, but the American and Canadian models of the Interstate were full-power versions. For the year 2000, Honda Australia imported the Valkyrie Interstate offering one colour only – Pearl Coronado Blue, with Pearl Twilight Silver. The Australian version had the European model's gearbox ratios and the exhaust system that was fitted to the European Standard F6C (with the smaller bore 15 mm tail pipes), which meant the silencer fell short of the end of the panniers. The normal side reflectors were omitted from the front mudguard and were a blank on the side of each pannier.

## 2001 GL1500 CF-1 Interstate

The competition was still hanging in there with some slight improvements; the Harley-Davidson Electra Glide Classic had new Dunlop tyres specially developed for the big H-D, while Yamaha's Royale Star Venture had an all-new seat and wraparound backrest. For its final year, the 2001 GL1500 Valkyrie Interstate had one minor modification to its

An interesting part of the bikes – the owner's manuals. The box is the Valkyrie's press pack along with the 'accessorised' Valkyrie single sheet brochure.

side-stand switch. Honda again maintained its prices for the Interstate and offered two new two-tone colours along with solid black; they were black with Pearl Cheyenne Red and black with Pearl Chaparral Beige. In Australia, Honda continued to offer the Interstate, but the only colour option was the black with Pearl Cheyenne Red.

Capacity at Honda's Marysville, Ohio, factory was shrinking due to an array of new models being built, including the new GL1800 Gold Wing and the 2002 VTX1800C, which would be produced in three versions. Something had to give way. With the Interstate's short life of only three model years, and with sales slowly petering out, it was discontinued.

By this time Honda was committed to the Harley look-alike machines of the Shadow and VTX series and by the following year the smaller VTX1300 would go into production, leaving even the standard Valkyrie vulnerable.

# Specifications

GL1500 Valkyrie Interstate 1999–2001

### Description Code
| | |
|---|---|
| Engine | SC41E |
| Frame | SC41 |

### Dimensions
| | |
|---|---|
| Overall length | 2,660 mm (104.7 inches) |
| Overall width | 970 mm (38.2 inches) |
| Overall height | 1,490 mm (58.7 inches) |
| Wheel base | 1,690 mm (66.5 inches) |
| Ground clearance | 150 mm (5.9 inches) |
| Seat height | 728 mm (28.7 inches) |

### Weight
| | |
|---|---|
| Dry weight | 351 kg (774 lbs) |
| | 352 kg (776 lbs) Californian Model |

### Engine
| | |
|---|---|
| Bore and stroke | 71.0 x 64.0 mm (2.8 x 2.5 inches) |
| Compression ratio | 9.8:1 |
| Displacement | 1,520cc (92.7 cubic-inches) |
| Carburettors | 6 x 28 mm diaphragm type CV Keihin |
| Fuel tank capacity | 26 litres (5.7 imperial gallons, 6.9 US gallons) |
| Power output | 106 bhp at 6,000 rpm |
| | 100 bhp at 6,000 rpm (Australian Model) |

| Power transmission | | US. Spec | Australian Spec |
|---|---|---|---|
| Primary reduction | | 1.591 | 1.591 |
| Secondary reduction | | 0.971 | 0.939 |
| Gear ratio | 1st. | 2.666 | 2.666 |
| | 2nd. | 1.722 | 1.722 |
| | 3rd. | 1.291 | 1.291 |
| | 4th. | 1.000 | 0.964 |
| | 5th. | 0.805 | 0.805 |
| Final reduction | | 2.833 | 2.833 |

## Chassis and suspension

| | | |
|---|---|---|
| Castor | | 32.2 degrees |
| Trail | | 152 mm (6.0 inches) |
| Tyre size | Front | 150/80 R17 72H |
| | Rear | 180/70 R16 77H |

## Electrical

| | |
|---|---|
| Battery | 12v–20AH |
| Generator output | 546 watts |

# 5

# Rune: From Concept to Reality

## 2004 NRX1800 DA/DB/EA/EB-4 (MEC) and 2005 NRX1800 DA/DB/EA/EB-5

Concept vehicles are generally just that; every year manufacturers all over the world produce them just to give the public a chance to see what their designers and engineers are dreaming up for the future. Some parts of the vehicle may one day enter production and others just never get made.

In 1995 at the Tokyo Motor Show, Honda unveiled a concept machine with a 1,500cc V-twin engine called the Zodia. This radical, innovative concept cruiser was a high-tech custom; the engine featured hydraulically driven camshafts that were designed to be maintenance free. Power transfer to the rear wheel was via hydro-mechanical automatic transmission – the Human Fitting Transmission (HFT). An oil cooler fitted between the front fork legs, just under the headlamp, was all part of the bike's styling elements. The braking system was an electronically enhanced version of the Combined Braking System and Anti-lock Braking System (CBS-ABS) from the ST1100 Pan European, with each disc brake-mounted to the rim of each wheel and the rear solid looking wheel being carried by a single-sided swingarm. The lines of the Zodia had classic retro elements that blended with new-age futuristic styling, including the flared sweeping mudguards and fully chromed twin exhaust featuring fishtail ends, which enhanced that custom look. The rear suspension was mounted directly under the single 1950s-looking saddle; up front was a very raked trailing-link fork system with concealed shock absorber in the steering head. The Zodia never went into production but some of the engine's outer design elements can be seen in the VTX cruisers.

In the mid-1990s, Honda was looking at different kinds of 'Custom Cruiser' machines and trying to invent a different aspect to the market where traditional cruisers were generally V-twins. Just after the launch of the GL1500 Valkyrie/F6C, Honda started work on some new concept machines just to gauge public feeling towards the Custom market. The T-series project was intended to push the boundaries beyond the normal limits – not just in design, but in engineering and production terms as well. These Concept machines were codenamed Concept Type 1, Type 2, Type 3 and Type 4. All the T-series concept bikes

The 1995 Honda concept, the 'Zodia' – a long and elegantly shaped Cruiser. (American Honda)

'T1', the low-slung GL1500 Valkyrie inspired concept. (American Honda)

'T2', the Neo/Retro-looking concept machine that Honda built as the 'Rune'. (American Honda)

came from ideas and sketches from designers at Honda Research & Development Americas (HRA) and each machine was built by them too, although HRA did have some outside help, which included a master fabricator who wasn't connected to the motorcycling industry in any way at all; again, the remit was 'push the boundaries'.

Concept Type 1 (T1) was a beautifully engineered machine painted in bright yellow, using a GL1500 engine, with a totally modified Valkyrie steel frame. The engine was a fuel-injected 1,520cc opposed-six, fitted with year 2000 Gold Wing chrome rocker-box covers, along with a single-piece chrome cam-belt cover found on the Valkyrie. The exhaust was a large bore, straight chromed turn-out, three-into-one each side.

The T1 concept was awash with chrome; everything was chrome or yellow paint work except for the black single seat, but even that had yellow flutes on each side. The front suspension was similar to that on the Valkyrie, while the rear single shock absorber was mounted under the seat and fuel tank. The cast aluminium swingarm attached to the specially made three-spoke rear wheel, along with the short stubby rear mudguard that incorporated a flush-mounted triple LED rear light unit, set the rear of the bike off with a clean, uncluttered look. The inverted front forks were wide in the chromed top and bottom yokes giving that 'custom' look from the front. A single gauge (speedometer) was mounted on the top yoke in front of the unusually positioned handlebars, which were fitted forward of the front forks, virtually flat but swept back.

'T3', the 'Hot Rod' GL1500-engined concept with chain-drive. (American Honda)

'T4', a pure Drag-Strip concept that couldn't be built. (American Honda)

The NRX1800 has the longest wheelbase of any Honda ever produced.

The T1 concept was first shown to the public late in 1998 and was designed to evoke a hot rod or muscle car image as the bike appeared very low to the ground.

Concept Type 2 (T2) used an all-aluminium frame with single-sided swingarm. The engine was a horizontally opposed six-cylinder with a cubic capacity of 1,832, similar to the GL1800 Gold Wing unit. The bike's design was neo/retro, evocative of roadsters from the 1940s and '50s, with its low and chopped look and deep mudguards, along with its long low-slung fuel tank. The exhaust system with huge chrome covers each side was short in order to keep the rear of the machine clean and unencumbered, showing the beautiful lines of the rear mudguard and fully chromed rear wheel, complete with a knock-off wheel hub on the left, while the right-hand side showed the massive swingarm with chrome cover over the differential; also visible was the single drilled disc. The retro-styled chrome rocker-box covers looked like pressed-steel units that would have been found on an old car engine; above these were chrome covers for the injectors and above them was the fuel tank; the tank itself was long, flowing under the single seat. The designers looked back at the Zodia's front suspension for inspiration when designing T2, and so the T2 concept used a very stylish twin-shock trailing-link suspension system with a complex mechanical presence, keeping in with that neo/retro look. The rear single-sided Pro Arm swingarm complete with mono-shock kept the rear uncluttered.

The headlight was a unique design featuring dual bulbs, one above the other; a projector beam in the lower section gave the unit a very different look, with the headlight shell colour matched to the bike and a chrome cap finishing it off nicely. T2's amazing handlebars were wing-shaped and incorporated digital instrumentation, leading them to be very stylish and futuristic; T2 cleverly blended future technology with its neo/retro looks.

Concept Type 3 (T3), like Type 1 (T1), was again based on the GL1500 engine, but fuel-injected. This bike was more of a hot rod machine from the 1950s with its flame-style paintwork along with its large 230/60-16 profile rear tyre. T3 had an elegantly designed exhaust system featuring six individual up-swept pipes, with elaborately bent header pipes. T3 was designed using a steel frame, a mono-shock rear suspension system, and very basic aluminium side covers; the interesting thing with this bike was the fact that it was chain-drive, so the designers converted the horizontally opposed six-cylinder engine to chain-drive, which was on the opposite side to where the shaft normally is with GL1500s. The long narrow radiator went from the underside of the headstock to the bottom of the engine, with a long air-scoop underneath it that protruded to the front of the bike and flowed all the way under the engine to just past the rear tyre. The bodywork was simple, with front mudguard, fuel tank and single-piece rear cowl attached to the frame and a single seat. The inverted front forks carried a chrome-plated front wheel with twin-disc brakes; the discs were nearly the size of the rims, bolted to the wheel's five spokes, and this

One of the most complex leading front forks ever fitted to a Honda production motorcycle, as well as the largest disc brake.

The Rune's fully chromed front suspension; note the shock absorbers behind the headlamp.

The ignition switch just under the fuel tank. To the front is the lever for the steering lock.

The chrome switchgear was minimal but set off with the chrome handlebar grips, brake and clutch fluid reservoirs.

Not the normal engine kill switch for a Honda, but for the Valkyrie Rune, nicely designed.

With the Valkyrie Rune's short silencers, Honda had to get exhaust volume; they achieved this with complicated cross-over pipes.

unusual design gave the front of the bike an open and airy appearance. On the rear was a single disc. Air-scoops just under the fuel tank were similar to T2's, long and curved. The handlebars were narrow and flat, designed to give the rider a 'lean forward' feel, and in the line of vison was a single gauge – the speedometer.

Concept Type 4 (T4) was the most outrageous concept of them all for a possible production machine, which, according to Honda, 'wasn't buildable'. The first three concepts were designer-driven, but for T4 Honda got master fabricator Mike McCluskey involved. He was renowned for restoring Ford Cobras and vintage aircraft through his own company. T4 was pure 'drag-strip' and built as a technical material study, using materials that wouldn't normally be used in a production motorcycle, and was a rolling exercise in construction techniques.

Solid Billet aluminium was a key ingredient in building this bike – the twin-spar frame alone was made out of seven sections, including the head-stock, which were almost seamlessly welded together. The three-piece swingarm was also milled pieces of Billet. The intriguing final shaft drive was mounted out-board of the swingarm because the rear tyre was so wide – a massive 26.0 x 9.0-15. The engine was based on the GL1500s unit and was again fuel-injected with newly fabricated rocker-covers, which with the red insert set them off. The sharply raked inverted front fork gave an airy appearance between the front wheel and the engine; this gave space for the hand-formed aluminium air-dam that housed the radiator, and a very neat and stylish coolant reservoir was located on the right-hand side of the engine. The beautifully straight three-into-one slash-cut exhaust system fitted to each side had pipes of the same length, giving an offset appearance when looked at from above. The long low seat with rear hump was designed for the forward lean feel with the footrests set much further back than normal and narrow flat handlebars. T4 was clean, simple and uncluttered, with Mike paying attention to detail by using flush-mounted hexagonal bolts. The finished look of the frame was brushed aluminium and then clear-coat lacquered. Like T1 and T3, T4 used a single instrument on the handlebars, with additional gauges between the fuel tank and the seat. The fuel tank was very small and perched on top of the frame.

Three of the T-series machines (T1, T2 and T3), all painted yellow, were displayed at the *Cycle World* motorcycle show in Long Beach, California, in December 2000 to gauge the public's reaction. When Honda's representatives talked to the public they got a good sense about all of the T-series bikes; the conservative motorcyclist went for T1, while the hot rod types steered more toward T3, although the out and out winner was surely T2, being nearly four times as popular than the other concepts. 'What did surprise us was the huge majority of people that liked the T2 concept', said Tony Schroeder, a senior Honda designer.

Masanori Aoki, who became Large Project Leader (LPL) for the Valkyrie Rune, remembers one person at the show saying 'I will bring $30,000 in cash, so please sell it to me right away', and some expressed opinions that T2 could never be built. For Honda, this became the challenge – to turn this concept into a mass production motorcycle without changing its appearance.

The challenge began when the designers and the engineers joined forces; the designers insisted this motorcycle had to be built to look the same as the concept, but the engineers felt changes would need to be made for production, engineering and legal reasons. Masanori Aoki (LPL) had to approach this new project differently. Normally the process would start with sketches and drawings, making parts from them, but with the Valkyrie Rune project

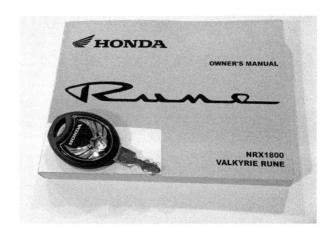

A special key for a special motorcycle, and a 2004 owner's manual.

A 2004 NRX 1800 Valkyrie Rune in Bloodstone Red Metallic.

For 2005 Honda used the same three colours as 2004. This 2005 NRX1800 with chrome wheel option is in Double Clear-Coat Black.

This model has after-market rear pillion footboards fitted. The Rune was designed for a solo rider.

The Valkyrie Rune is just stunning with beautifully designed rocker-box covers and exhaust down-pipes.

the bike was already virtually built, so to get this to a running and functional motorcycle they had to engineer parts to fit the concept. 'As an engineer, I thought the process was completely backward' said Aoki. The Rune's engine wasn't a problem as the basics were a GL1800, but that's where its association ends. The only other Honda motorcycle the Rune had any association with was the RC211V GP race-bikes; its rear suspension was developed for the race bikes. The Pro-Link unit was a bit unconventional as the top mount for the suspension was contained within the swingarm; this gave great benefits to the Valkyrie Rune's low seat height of just 27.2 inches (691 mm). Honda's designers intended the Valkyrie Rune to be a solo motorcycle with its single gunslinger seat and rearward seating position. The suspension system, having no top frame-mount, meant that there was reduced negative suspension energy being transmitted to the frame, giving more optimum frame rigidity. This in turn gave better handling in corners. The Rune was the longest (in wheelbase terms) motorcycle Honda had ever built; from axle to axle it measured 68.9 inches (1750 mm), which is 2.36 inches (60 mm) longer than the GL1800 Gold Wing.

Aoki gave us the first touring motorcycle with an aluminium frame and now it was the turn of the cruisers. The Rune's huge aluminium diamond-shape frame was unique, having its own style with the engine being a stress-member with sub-frames running alongside the engine. A rear sub-frame was steel and carried the ginormous rear mudguard.

Using the horizontally opposed six-cylinder engine gave the Rune a low centre-of-gravity, despite the long seamless 6.1 US gallons teardrop fuel tank being in the conventional place.

*Above left*: The headlamp, with its colour-matched base, chrome cap and visor, was designed to complement the exhaust system.

*Above right*: The Rune was the first Honda motorcycle to use LED rear lights – nine in each unit.

The Valkyrie Rune's engine displacement was 1,832cc, liquid-cooled with fuel-injection. The six 32 mm synchronised throttle bodies delivered air to the six twelve-hole programmed fuel-injectors which were specially designed by Denso; these produced an atomised fuel mixture that gave optimum efficiency and power. For maximum engine performance, Honda fitted a 6.9-litre air-box that supplied cool, clean air to the engine. Although Honda wouldn't give any performance figures for the Rune, an American magazine dyno-tested one and came up with a power output of 90.6 bhp at 5,250 rpm, and a torque figure of 110.9 ft/lbs at a very low 2,500 rpm. Cylinder head design used parallel two-valves per cylinder, which meant that the valves were at the top of each cylinder head, as opposed to one at the top and one at the bottom. Aoki designed the heads like this on the GL1800; the heads were chamfered to allow the rider's feet to fit underneath, so making it impossible to have the rear cylinder's exhaust valve at the bottom of the head. To boost power, valve actuation was via shim-under-bucket, which needed no initial servicing (600 miles) but did need its first valve adjustment at 32,000 miles.

Starting the Rune was simple – put the key in the ignition and push the starter button and let the Rotary Air Control Valve (RACV) system do the rest. This provided the bike with automatic-choke, to maintain the precise idle speed when cold. The cooling system featured two radiators, one on top of the other, with twin cooling fans, one on each side of the top radiator. They dispersed the heat through vents between the radiator and fuel-injection chrome covers. The beautifully sculptured chrome radiator grill was reminiscent of a classic roadster style from the 1950s, with colour-matched surround.

All in all, Honda created more than eleven new technologies that had to be adapted to put the Valkyrie Rune into production. One headache for Masanori Aoki was the exhaust system; this short stubby system was not to be changed, but how to make it so noise wasn't a problem? With each exhaust measuring just over a metre in length from front to rear this was proving to be difficult; to keep noise levels within the legal limits it needed volume. On the surface the system looks simple, but underneath it is very complex; to overcome the problem with its lack of volume Aoki engineered the system with the two rear cylinder

The Rune had five-spoke wheels with two options available – silver (Spec47) or chrome.

down-pipes crossing over each other at the rear of the engine, just in front of the rear suspension, with a balance pipe between the ends of each silencer, behind the suspension.

The Rune's main feature was also very complex. The fully chrome-plated trailing-link front suspension axle load was transferred via pushrods and linkages to two upper shock absorbers. One had a main spring, while the other had a sub-spring and damping system; this suspension system was inspired by the Honda Zodia Concept motorcycle from 1995. The Valkyrie Rune's suspension system on both the front and the rear offered 3.9 inches (99 mm) of travel, making the ride firm, compliant and with excellent stability.

When riding a Rune, the beautiful sculptured headlamp seems a long way away with its chrome cap and colour-matched bottom cover. The design of the unit was to complement the Rune's exhaust system with its shape; the interesting thing Honda did with this reflector-type headlamp was to place its low-beam on the top of the unit while the main beam was in the lower section.

Huge neo/retro-looking front and rear mudguards curved around the wheels, giving the bike a ground-hugging appearance. The rear mudguard featured two low, flush, vertically mounted, clean-looking rear light units, which housed the stop/tail lamps – each containing nine LEDs. The chrome rear turn signals flared out of each side of the rear mudguard; from a birds-eye perspective these also complemented the exhaust design. With this motorcycle, chrome was the order of the day with its very basic switch gear all chrome plated, along with each master cylinder for brakes and clutch, as well as levers and grips.

A powerful cruiser requires powerful brakes and the Valkyrie Rune had the largest disc brakes ever fitted to a production Honda motorcycle. The front dual discs were 330 mm in diameter with three-piston callipers each side. The rear was 336 mm single disc with a twin-piston calliper. The braking system was a combined one with the front brake lever operating the two outer pistons in each front calliper; the rear brake pedal operated the two rear pistons and the middle in each of the front callipers through a Proportional Control Valve (PCV). Honda built the Rune as a radical custom machine and spared no expense; the brake and clutch hoses along with the throttle cables were covered with stainless steel mesh. The oil dipstick was also stainless steel, machined for that custom look and with great attention to detail.

The instruments were in two places, with the information lights – such as neutral, oil temperature, lock and HISS – and high-beam lights mounted in the handlebar clamp along with the trip set switch and illumination switch. This altered the brightness of the multi-function display and had six settings, while the LCD speedo (which could display either KPH or MPH), the odometer and fuel gauge were located in the chrome panel on top of the fuel tank, which also incorporated the fuel filler cap. Honda developed the most complex steering lock imaginable for the Rune. Like the exhaust system, on the surface it looked simple, but underneath it was anything but. To lock the steering all that was needed was to turn the handlebars to the left and pull the lock lever (located near the ignition switch); to unlock the steering just turn the ignition on, which sounds straightforward. The actual operation of the lock was via a Steering Lock Unit located near the steering stem; this unit was linked with the engine control module (ECM) and the ignition key. To the Rune, Honda fitted their Honda Ignition Security System (HISS), which was linked to the ECM, therefore before unlocking the steering of the Rune, the ignition key (which was fitted with a transponder) and ECM had to match their codes. Once the ignition was

With the Valkyrie Rune nothing is simple – even the seat lock mechanism is complicated.

switched on, a signal was sent to the ECM and to the Steering Lock Unit's solenoid, which then released the lock.

Cosmetic changes from the T2 Concept to the production Valkyrie Rune were very few; the winged handlebars had to go along with the rear wheel centre spinner and the projector-beam headlight, but, conversely, substantial front engine protectors that weren't on T2 were added to the Rune.

So what is Rune? Honda wanted to keep the Valkyrie's mystical heritage running; they said that the Rune stemmed from the heart of the Valkyrie's soul and was created in the very fires of imagination. Runes are letters carved into mystical stones or wood from the ancient northern European, Germanic alphabet.

Four versions of the Honda Valkyrie Rune were offered with different options on the wheels and handlebars. One unit came with silver painted wheels with 'Forward-Set' or 'Rear-Set' handlebars; the difference was the 'Rear-Set' handlebars were 20 mm lower and 50 mm further back than the 'Forward-Set', these units were referred to as Spec47. The other options were with chrome wheels, again with the different handlebar setup.

The same three colours were offered in America for both model years – Pearl Chromium Purple (commonly known as Illusion Blue), Bloodstone Red Metallic (Candy Black Cherry), and black (Double Clear-Coat Black), while the only other country to have the Valkyrie

The Rune's instrumentation surrounded by chrome plating.

Rune – Canada – had Pearl Chromium Purple for 2004 and Bloodstone Red Metallic for 2005.

The Rune was American-designed and American-built in Marysville, Ohio, with production starting on 22 April 2003. Although this bike was an unusual machine, it was still built on the same production line as the Gold Wing, VTX1800, and VT1100. American Honda set a price for the Spec47 units at $24,499; for the chrome-wheeled models the price was $26,999. Although only marketed officially in two countries, Honda Motor Co. Ltd in Japan did show the Valkyrie Rune to the public at the 37th Tokyo Motor Show in October 2003. It was dubbed 'Japan Premiere', but was only an exhibition model. Vice President of the Motorcycle Division for American Honda, Ray Blank, told the media that no more than 1,200 Runes were to be built; he also stated that 'American Honda will stand by its commitment not to increase production numbers to meet a likely greater demand, thus preserving its exclusivity'.

It's alright the manufacturer building the motorcycle, but what did the media think? US publication, *Rider*, had a studio picture of a Pearl Chromium Purple Rune on their May 2003 cover with a headline 'Rune with a view Honda's Awesome New Valkyrie Rune 1800 Six'. *Cycle World* in their March 2003 issue had a Bloodstone Red Metallic Rune on the cover saying 'HIGH STYLE! Low Volume' with a six-page article featuring some beautiful photographs taken by Brian Blades. *Motorcycle Cruiser* magazine, December 2002, ran

The Honda NRX1800 Valkyrie Rune, the Mona Lisa of motorcycles – the concept that became reality.

a two-page feature on the new 2004 Valkyrie Rune, written by Jamie Elvidge; although they just used Honda's press pictures for the feature, one picture showed the concept T2 in yellow on a lit plinth. Honda is said to have sold a yellow Rune to a customer in the States that was originally a test bike on Honda's fleet and used by motorcycle magazines. Originally black, the Rune was painted Pearl Yellow at the request of the customer, this was done at Honda's R&D department in Torrance, California. The September 2003 issue of *Motorcyclist* magazine ran their first test using a black Rune – 'Honda Rune. Big, Bad, Expensive... and Worth It!' The six-page test featured a 'Rune: Second Opinion' by the Editor-in-Chief, Mitch Boehm. He said he was lukewarm about the Rune with its ultra-high price and limited availability and that he thought it was a 'two-wheeled publicity stunt', but after Boehm had ridden a production Rune for a couple of days he was hooked, saying 'I'm a believer'. Similar feelings could have been said for other magazines too, with *Motorcycle Consumer News* declaring 'Outrageous!' on the front cover of their October 2003 issue. The Honda Valkyrie Rune won its first award in *Motorcycle Cruiser*'s October 2003 issue; they declared the Rune 'Cruiser of the Year' and presented Honda with a mythical sword in stone trophy. Over the following eight pages they did a test 'Quest of the Rune' with a double-paged photograph from Kevin Wing of two Valkyrie Runes – one Pearl Chromium Purple, the other Bloodstone Red Metallic. The test also featured the concepts to the Rune.

American Honda produced an excellent eighteen-page sales brochure for the NRX1800 Valkyrie Rune with very little text, but many beautiful pictures. The first page showed

The sculptured radiator grill, reminiscent of the 1950s hot rod scene, along with the elegantly made engine guards.

a black Rune in front of a mythical backdrop. The following pages were action shots featuring a red Rune; nicely chosen locations for other still images were spooky and eerie, giving a mystical feel, and the last couple of pages showed detailed features of the Rune, along with colour choice, model variation and specifications.

This motorcycle wasn't cheap to buy and American Honda wanted the customers who bought the Rune to feel they had bought something a bit special. Each buyer of the NRX1800 Valkyrie Rune was given a special book presented in its own leather-bound box, embossed with the Rune logo. Part of the book's front cover and all of the back was leather bound, while the other section of the cover was a painted piece of steel incorporating the fuel tank decal; the books were published in each of the Rune's three colours so whichever colour Rune was purchased, the book matched. Opening the heavy front cover revealed that it was actually little more than the sales brochure, although it did have additional pages showing some design sketches of the bike and slightly extended text. Attached to the inside rear cover were two CD-ROMs – one featuring the service manual, owner's manual and the rune television commercial, the other containing the 2004 press information on the Rune with numerous pictures and information. Every book supplied came with a personally signed letter from the then Vice President of the

The Valkyrie Rune brochure, along with the special owner's book, complete with CD-ROMs and a letter from Ray Blank.

Motorcycle Division for American Honda, Ray Blank. In the letter, Mr Blank explained that the Rune was 'one of the most important and visionary motorcycles the world has ever seen'.

How should one describe the Valkyrie Rune? Some people don't like it, others like it as a motorcycle, and some don't really think of it as a motorcycle, but as a work of art. I would agree – it's an amazing machine and Honda were very brave to have built something like the Rune. At the time, what would have been the Valkyrie Rune's competition? Nothing at all in mass production terms, this was a custom-built machine, built by the world's number one manufacturer. To change or add anything to a Valkyrie Rune would be like painting a pair of spectacles on the Mona Lisa – this motorcycle is indeed a masterpiece. Honda built something that is unique and special, and as they say, that's 'The Power of Dreams'.

## Specifications

NRX1800 Valkyrie Rune 2004–2005

Description Code
| | |
|---|---|
| Engine | SC53E |
| Frame | SC53 |

Dimensions
| | |
|---|---|
| Overall length | 2,560 mm (100.8 inches) |
| Overall width | 920 mm (36.2 inches) |
| Overall height | 1,090 mm (42.9 inches) ... Model equipped with taller handlebars. |
| | 1,070 mm (42.1 inches) ... Model equipped with lower handlebars. |

| | |
|---|---|
| Wheel base | 1,750 mm (68.9 inches) |
| Ground clearance | 135 mm (5.3 inches) |
| Seat height | 690 mm (27.2 inches) |

Weight

| | |
|---|---|
| Dry weight | 368 kg (811 lbs) |
| | 369 kg (813 lbs) Californian Model |

Engine

| | |
|---|---|
| Bore and stroke | 74.0 x 71.0 mm (2.91 x 2.80 inches) |
| Compression ratio | 9.8:1 |
| Displacement | 1,832cc (111.8 cubic-inches) |
| Carburetion | 6 x 32 mm throttle bodies, PGM-FI with automatic choke |
| Fuel tank capacity | 23 litres (5.08 imperial gallons, 6.1 US gallons) |
| Power output | Not available from Honda |

| Power transmission | | US. Spec |
|---|---|---|
| Primary reduction | | 1.591 |
| Secondary reduction | | 1.028 |
| Gear Ratio, | 1st. | 1.944 |
| | 2nd. | 1.347 |
| | 3rd. | 1.035 |
| | 4th. | 0.843 |
| | OD. | 0.705 |
| Final reduction | | 2.917 |

Chassis and suspension

| | | |
|---|---|---|
| Castor | | 29.0 degrees |
| Trail | | 125 mm (4.9 inches) |
| Tyre size | Front | 150/60 R18M/C 67V |
| | Rear | 180/55 R17M/C 73V |

Electrical

| | |
|---|---|
| Battery | 12v–18AH |
| Generator output | 959 watts |

# 6

# Gold Wing Valkyrie/F6C

## 2014 GL1800 C-E and 2015 GL1800 C-F (MJR)

The new GL1800 Gold Wing Valkyrie/F6C launched in November 2013 wasn't in fact that new. The engine and Diamond-type frame technology was some fourteen years old, although the frame's headstock had been altered to give the bike a castor angle of 29 degrees 50' and a trail of 114 mm (4.5 inches) as opposed to the Gold Wing Tourer version's castor angle of 29 degrees 15' and trail of 109 mm (4.3 inches). Altering the frame in this way increased the new Valkyrie/F6C's wheelbase by 15 mm (0.6 inches) to 1,705 mm (67.1 inches). The rear sub-frame was new and the engine support beams' rigidity balance was subtly adjusted by making them softer; these in turn improved rider feel through the chassis. The 260.6 lbs (118.2 kg) engine was the same as that of the Tourer and F6B, (so no 'hotting-up' this time) – a 1,832cc liquid-cooled horizontally opposed six-cylinder with a bore and stroke of 74 x 71 mm (2.91 x 2.80 inches), as well as single overhead camshafts with two valves per cylinder and with the same compression ratio of 9.8:1. Fuel delivery was by a Programmed Fuel Injection (PGM-FI) system with six high-pressure programmed fuel injectors for excellent metering under varying conditions. Honda improved the stability of the naked Gold Wing Valkyrie/F6C by evenly balancing weight distribution front to rear; this was virtually even, with a weight bias of 49.9/50.1 respectively. According to *Cycle World* magazine, when they put the GL1800 Gold Wing Valkyrie through its paces, comparing it with a Ducati Diavel Carbon, they dyno-tested the bikes and the Valkyrie produced 101.7 bhp at 5,330 rpm and 111.7 ft/lbs of torque at 3,920 rpm.

The reason given for the development of the Gold Wing Valkyrie/F6C was to give younger riders the experience of riding a machine that wasn't as daunting as a fully dressed GL1800 Gold Wing (weighing in at some 183 lbs (83 kg) lighter) and to appreciate the performance that a horizontally opposed six-cylinder could give. The engineers intended the Gold Wing Valkyrie/F6C to have a laid-back spirit in daily life while looking sharp on the streets. The bike's styling from the side gives the sense of 'kind-curved lines', from the top of the engine to around the headlamp, down over the fuel tank and seat, right down the rear mudguard. The design around the radiator area is very similar to that of a Ducati Diavel, which also has twin side-mounted radiators. Honda designers placed the air intake at the top of the

*Right*: 2014 UK GL1800 Gold Wing F6C, which had better specification than its American counterpart (the Valkyrie) as ABS was a standard feature.

*Below*: The Ducati has dual side-mounted radiators like the Gold Wing Valkyrie/F6C. This bike must have given Honda some influence in its design.

*Above*: The right-hand bike shows the lock for the fuel tank flap, while the left-hand bike shows the slash-cut silencers.

*Left*: The large sculptured rear passenger grab handles can be removed along with the passenger seat for a solo ride. Honda offered colour-matched rear mudguard lids as an accessory to cover up the holes.

radiator; this created a backward air flow, and in turn diverted warm air away from the rider. Viewing the Valkyrie/F6C from the front/side angle, it looked more aggressive with the radiator cowl protruding to the front of the bike, giving it its own personality. The 1800 Valkyrie/F6C was the first Gold Wing to use LED lighting; the headlight was designed to give the Valkyrie/F6C its own character and unique face design. The LED headlamp used separate vertical divided reflectors for its main and low beams; this in turn was to create a mechanical look. The headlight itself turned night into day. Uniquely positioned air ducts beside the headlamp were designed to allow fresh air to feed the twin 40 mm throttle bodies via the 6.6-litre airbox and complement the fork covers. The rear tail light was neatly fitted flush in the rear mudguard, with the rear turn signals mounted just behind. The rear light and turn signals were also LED; the only problem with this sort of lighting is that when it fails, the complete unit must be replaced.

The Honda Gold Wing Valkyrie/F6C's downward shape was designed to 'create a vibrant and elegant curvaceous figure', in Honda's words.

The LCD instrumentation of the Valkyrie/F6C; note the ignition switch in the tank top chrome bezel.

The contours of the 5.04 imperial gallons (22.9 litres, 6.05 US gallons) fuel tank had a large shrouded area at the front, was slim at the rear, along with the two-piece low, 300 mm wide seat, with a height of 734 mm (28.9 inches), which viewed from the top of the bike gave a sense of an elegant curvaceous figure.

Honda used lengthened 45 mm telescopic fork legs to raise the front end, which incorporated a cartridge damper, while the rear had a Honda Multi-Action System (HMAS) mono-shock that could be adjusted manually via the dial located on the left-hand side in front of the battery. This was for spring pre-load; both the front and rear spring and damping rates were modified to complement the Valkyrie/F6C's reduction in weight and give the bike a plusher, yet well controlled feel. The rear aluminium swingarm was the same as the GL1800 Gold Wing's – a single-sided unit with the suspension working through a Pro-Link system.

One interesting thing was that the designers went back to the original GL1000 Gold Wing wheel diameters, with the beautifully made ten-spoke cast wheels – 19 inches at the front, 17 inches at the rear, the front featured hollow spokes to make the wheel lighter and stronger. The tyres fitted were tubeless Dunlop Sportmax Radials – 130/60R-19 at the front, while the rear wore a 180/55R-17. This, along with the longer forks, helped increase the ground clearance to 145 mm (5.7 inches), as opposed to the Tourer Gold Wing's 125 mm (4.9 inches).

For some reason Honda kept the braking system on the Valkyrie simple and straightforward; while the rear had a three-piston calliper, each front calliper had four pistons per unit. The two 310-mm floating front discs were controlled via the handlebar lever, with the 316-mm rear ventilated disc brake being operated via the foot pedal. For the Gold Wing Valkyrie/F6C models with ABS, Honda used a two-channel Anti-Lock Braking System for a safer stopping experience in slippery conditions.

The exhaust system was designed short and featured the Honda Evolution Catalysing System 3 (HECS3); this employed a three-way catalytic process, reducing the volume of harmful gases released into the atmosphere. The designers focused on the exhaust sound, which gave the Valkyrie/F6C a meaner growl, with the tailpipe being slash-cut to show three small pipes in each silencer helping enhance the sound. The two silencers were different sizes, with the left-hand unit's volume being 3.8 litres, while the right was just 3.3 litres. The Honda engineers prototyped ten different exhaust systems; they were searching for the perfectly balanced exhaust note and wanted it to have a dual personality, with a throaty growl in the lower rpm range and more of a high-pitch crescendo at the maximum range.

From the back note the small pipes from each silencer, six pipes for a six-cylinder machine.

*Above*: The side-cover emblems of the F6C; on the American bike the emblem says 'Valkyrie'.

*Left*: The UK-specification F6C was one of the first Honda UK bikes to be equipped with the indicators as running lights. All the lighting on the Valkyrie/F6C was LED.

The lockable under-seat luggage compartment that stores the owner's manual and tool kit.

The instrumentation was a self-contained unit using some of the Gold Wing Tourer's features such as the opening and closing ceremonies, which could either be personalised or not used at all as the function was optional. In 'NR' (Normal) display there was no opening ceremony. When the function was set to 'SP' (Special) mode, however, switching on the ignition showed an opening ceremony including the words Gold Wing and Valkyrie (or F6C in Europe and Japan); this was the only time that 'Gold Wing' was mentioned on the bike as there were no Gold Wing emblems anywhere. Honda made the multi-function digital LCD instrumentation compact but it still incorporated a bar tachometer, fuel gauge, odometer (which doubled up as a tripometer, Trip A and Trip B) and a clock. They also came with a backlight brightness facility with five settings. The information lights were turn signals, HISS (not American models), PGM-FI, high coolant temperature indicator, oil pressure, main beam and ABS; situated on each side of these indicator lights were the select button to the left and the set button to the right. The steering lock was incorporated into the ignition switch located just in front of the fuel filler cap flap, which was part of a large chrome bezel.

Compared with the other two Gold Wing models, the Gold Wing Valkyrie/F6C used a totally different handlebar setup, with a 25.4 mm (1 inch) diameter, single tubular steel unit, as opposed to the cast aluminium units fitted to the other two bikes. The bars were set 33 mm (1.3 inch) forward, 38 mm (1.5 inch) higher and were wider

A 2015 fortieth anniversary Gold Wing F6C in the best colour for the UK – Candy Prominence Red.

by 18 mm (0.7 inch) compared to the Gold Wing Tourer and F6B. Honda also fitted rubber mounts to the handlebars for added comfort. The switchgear was very basic with the right-hand unit featuring a hazard warning switch, along with the kill and starter switches. The left had the normal main and low beam, horn and turn signal switches. Honda improved the hydraulic clutch lever's pull ratio by offering a lighter action; the load was reduced by 60 newtons.

In the States, Honda offered the Gold Wing Valkyrie in two versions and three colour options, which were Graphite Black, Bordeaux Red Metallic, and Atmosphere Blue Metallic. The Atmosphere Blue-coloured bike came with black-out engine, along with black chrome fuel tank bezel and headlamp cap. The passenger grab handles were also black rather than the silver of the other two colours. The option of Anti-Lock brakes (ABS) was available, but only if buying a Graphite Black Valkyrie. For the three colours the price was $17,999, but adding a $1,000 for the ABS version. Buyers could also customise their Gold Wing Valkyrie/ F6C with Honda's genuine accessories. A total of fifteen were available, from windscreens to leather saddlebags.

Honda UK imported the Gold Wing F6C in two colour options – Graphite Black and the Bordeaux Red Metallic. Both were fitted with ABS and HISS, which was standard throughout Europe, but for a bike with a fourteen-year-old engine the price was just too expensive at £18,399.

'Venture in to the unknown' – that's what Honda did with the Valkyrie/F6C, but it only lasted two model years.

Unfortunately, the Valkyrie/F6C was destined to fail, which, for the designers, must be so disheartening; younger riders couldn't afford the bike, which was one of the designers' main aims – to get them riding one of these, then they may progress to the 'Touring' version of the Gold Wing later, but it didn't work. The other problem was the marketing; generally, with a new bike Honda would do individual sales brochures to promote the bike with its features and benefits, but for some reason in Europe this didn't happen. The bike was quietly listed in Full Range or Custom brochures along with other bikes and was left to sell itself, only it didn't – the bike was too expensive for what it was and only lasted two model years in the developed world. In the modern world, everything seems to be black, with not a lot of chrome which is what the original Valkyrie was all about, a 'Custom Cruiser', whereas the new Gold Wing Valkyrie/F6C is more 'Cruiser' than 'Custom'.

Honda offered the Gold Wing Valkyrie/F6C again as a 2015 model; the Gold Wing series was celebrating its fortieth year of production, so as this bike was a Gold Wing Honda gave it a bit of treatment too... On one side of the ignition key Honda put the Gold Wing logo and '40th Anniversary'. In the States, a new colour – Candy Prominence Red – was the only colour offered, and no ABS version either, while in the UK Honda offered two colour options – Candy Prominence Red and Graphite Black, both coming with ABS brakes as standard.

Ironically, the 2014 Gold Wing Valkyrie/F6C appeared exactly thirty years after the demise of the last naked Gold Wing – the GL1200E standard.

For years, numerous Valkyrie/F6C owners had been crying out for Honda to build a new, more up-to-date Valkyrie/F6C, utilising modern components, but keeping the 'classic' styling. The problem with what Honda actually produced was that to some people the Gold Wing Valkyrie/F6C was neither a Gold Wing nor a Valkyrie/F6C; it certainly didn't have the panache of the original 1997 version. Unfortunately for both Honda themselves and Gold Wing/Valkyrie owners alike, the new bike wasn't the success story that they had all hoped for; perhaps one day Honda *will* realise the power of *our* dreams.

## Specifications

GL1800 Gold Wing Valkyrie/F6C

Description Code
| | |
|---|---|
| Engine | SC47E |
| Frame | SC68 |

Dimensions
| | |
|---|---|
| Overall length | 2,470 mm (97.2 inches) |
| Overall width | 940 mm (37.0 inches) |
| Overall height | 1,155 mm (45.5 inches) |
| Wheel base | 1,705 mm (67.1 inches) |
| Ground clearance | 145 mm (5.7 inches) |
| Seat height | 734 mm (28.9 inches) |

Weight
| | |
|---|---|
| Kerb weight | 342 kg (754 lbs) ABS model |
| | 340 kg (750 lbs) US Spec non-ABS |

Engine
| | |
|---|---|
| Bore and stroke | 74.0 x 71.0 mm (2.91 x 2.80 inches) |
| Compression ratio | 9.8:1 |
| Displacement | 1,832cc (111.8 cubic-inches) |
| Carburetion | 2 x 40 mm throttle bodies, PGM-FI with automatic choke |
| Fuel tank capacity | 22.9 litres (5.04 imperial gallons, 6.05 US gallons) |
| Power output | 115 bhp at 5,500 rpm (Valkyrie) |
| | 112 bhp at 5,500 rpm (F6C) |

Power transmission

| | | |
|---|---|---|
| Primary reduction | | 1.591 |
| Secondary reduction | | 1.028 |
| Gear ratio | 1st. | 2.375 |
| | 2nd. | 1.454 |
| | 3rd. | 1.068 |
| | 4th. | 0.843 |
| | 5th. | 0.685 |
| Final reduction | | 2.750 |

Chassis and suspension

| | | |
|---|---|---|
| Castor | | 29.5 degrees |
| Trail | | 114 mm (4.5 inches) |
| Tyre size | Front | 130/60 R19M/C 61H Dunlop D254F |
| | Rear | 180/55 R17M/C 73H Dunlop D256 |

Electrical

| | |
|---|---|
| Battery | 12v–20AH |
| Generator output | 1,100 watts |

# Acknowledgements

Honda Motor Co. Ltd Japan.
American Honda Motor Co. Inc.
*MotorCycle News* (MCN) for allowing me to reproduce the prototype article.

I would like to express my gratitude to the friendly and obliging motorcycle dealers that have helped me with the photographs for this book: Dan Anthony and Paul Julian from Bridge Motorcycles, Exeter; Matt Holmes and Andrew Hodges of Craigs Honda, Shipley; Russ Clay and Mark Herbert of DK Motorcycles limited, Newcastle-Under-Lyme; Steve Shaw and Ian Lacey of Highbarn Motorcycles, Chadderton, Oldham; David Silver of David Silver Spares for letting me take some photographs of the exhibits in his excellent Honda Museum.

Many thanks to Jacek Piterow for the stripe dimensions and his photographs as well as to Steve Tyrrell for his Valkyrie Interstate photographs.

And lastly, to Mana Maruyama (Warne) and Steven Warne for the 'Spirit of the Phoenix' translation from Japanese.

Special thanks to Wendy Rakestrow for helping me go through this process a second time.